THIS COPY OF

You Are Greater Than You Know

PRESENTED TO

Mrs. Ross Black

BY

Mrs. Ray Hill White

with warm wishes and high hopes that it may
be of help in achieving life's most priceless
treasures: an understanding heart, love of
friends, work that serves, inner peace, vigorous
health, a deeper, more satisfying life.

You Are Greater
Than You Know

You Are Greater Than You Know

Lou Austin

THE PARTNERSHIP FOUNDATION
WINCHESTER, VIRGINIA

First Printing, Sept., 1955
Second Printing, Oct., 1955

TO

MY PARTNER

IN GRATITUDE FOR LIFE,

FAMILY, FRIENDS, WORK,

HEALTH, COUNTRY—BUT

ABOVE ALL, FOR BEING

MY PARTNER

* * *

*"To whom much hath been given,
of him shall much be required."*

Introduction

EDWARD R. MURROW, in introducing the author of this book on his THIS I BELIEVE radio program, said: "Lou Austin was born in poverty and raised in an orphan asylum. For forty years he fought for success, money and position. Broke in 1932, he changed his whole philosophy of life and lived his new beliefs. All he had previously fought for and failed to get came to him. . ."

What you are about to read is written by a man who is not a worker in organized religion, welfare, or social service, but a business man who started with nothing and built an enterprise for which he recently refused more than a million dollars. Making a million has been done in America before, but in this case it was accomplished without sales effort or advertising.

I have seen him in action over many years in association with thousands of people. I have seen a part of the breadth and depth of his love for all kinds and conditions of men. And I have seen indisputable evidence that his system works.

So much love for mankind was contained in what he had to offer that his customers came back for more and brought their friends with them. He has come into a personal relationship with the Power that created him that seems to him so easy to understand that he has written this book to share his discovery with others. I rejoice that he has done this, and hope that it is the first of many writings of his that will multiply largely the spiritual forces that I have seen called forth, employed and proven richly resultful in his own wide circle of influence.

WILLIAM N. THOMAS, Rear Admiral, C.H.C.
U. S. Navy, Ret., Former Chief of Chaplains

Foreword

THIS BOOK was written for those who know there *must* be a better way of life than the one they are now living. It is by a business man who found that way in the workaday world. He tells in the first two chapters ("THE STORY" and "THE STORY BEHIND THE STORY") how this better way was found. If business details are uninteresting to you, you can skip these chapters without much loss. They were included only to give weight and authority to the way of life described in the rest of the book. You should know that this better way was not discovered in an "ivory tower" or a "sheltered cloister," but in the everyday affairs of the business world. We have been told that the book gives greater returns with the re-reading. It is hoped that this holds true for you.

Contents

	PAGE
INTRODUCTION	vii
FOREWORD	ix

THE TRUTH

THE STORY	1
THE STORY BEHIND THE STORY . . .	22
LIFE'S GREATEST DISCOVERY: GOD IS	
WITHIN YOU	54
You Are Greater Than You Know . .	58
What Are You?	60

THE WAY

BREATHE OUT EGO, BREATHE IN GOD . .	79
In Illness	93
When You Can't Sleep	96
In Frustration	101
In Anger	105
In Your Relations With Family	
and Friends	108
In Meeting With Success . . .	111
In Keeping Young and Well . . .	112
In Money Matters	116

THE LIFE

THE NEW TRUE YOU	125
TOO LATE, YOU SAY?	203

xi

THE TRUTH

The Story

THIS IS A STORY of two partners whom I came to know rather well. One was an ordinary person, going nowhere in particular until he met up with the other. With the help of his Partner, he came into valuable possessions and was widely regarded as a "successful man." People tend to worship success, so the ordinary person was often regarded with great respect, while his Partner, who was really responsible for the success, went unmentioned.

This story is to set the record of this Partnership straight, in the hope that others may find this simple path to real success. Here is a pattern for successful living which in my experience has been unfailing. It is a simple formula, available to all. The story that follows is true in every respect. I know. I am that ordinary person. I am the benefiting partner.

* * *

I came into property now worth over a million dollars, all because of a discovery so revolutionary and yet so simple that you may have trouble believing it. Ever since I made this tremendous discovery some 23 years ago, things have gravitated to me in a steady stream. And not just material things, the accumulation of which often does one's family more harm than good, but things of real value: love of friends, peace of mind, good health, and a very much deeper, more satisfying life.

Up to the time of the great discovery, I had been the typical white collar person, hoping and struggling to "rise in the world." I had been born in poverty and raised in an orphan asylum. All my notions of success had revolved around the usual standard of money, position, fame. At age 32, in pursuit of these things, I had got myself in a business tangle which threatened me with ruin and disgrace.

Nine years later (in 1932) I emerged as owner of the property involved, as yet unprofitable but offering great opportunity. I paused long enough to analyze the factors that had delivered me from disaster and presented me with so wonderful a promise. What I saw in my mind's eye was a huge jig-saw puzzle, all put together and containing every piece necessary to give me this opportunity. And I had not laid a single piece! For the first time in my life, I recognized that a power greater than my own was dominant in my affairs.

Out of this realization flowed the great discovery bringing with it a profound and revolutionary change for good, not only in my personal and family and business life but in an ever-widening circle of friends. It has proved so helpful that I feel an obligation to share it as widely as possible, and that is how this book came to be. But let me "brief" you on the highlights that led to the great discovery. I've numbered them so as to make it easy for you to check my part against my Partner's part in my affairs, when revealed later in The Story Behind The Story.

1.   The time of the discovery was July 1932, at about the bottom of the Depression. A company I had organized nine years before was about to be forced out of business.

2.   We had been lucky to keep going that long. In 1923, I had brought some friends together and organized a company; got a little over $100,000 capital and promptly paid out $50,000 for a 50 year contract to distribute water from a certain mineral spring said to possess (and it does) remarkable health-giving properties.

3.   Shortly thereafter I learned that the company to whom we paid the $50,000 had neither the right to make the contract nor to take the money, since it was in receivership at the time and its entire property was about to be foreclosed.

4.   Thus the contract for which I gave out $50,000 of my own and my friends' money was not worth the paper it was written on. That was not all.

5.   Almost all of the balance of our money had been invested in a bottling plant, bottles, cases, trucks and other equipment difficult to liquidate.

6.   Then I came across records of the Food & Drug Administration of the U. S. to the effect that the water we were about to distribute had been found "polluted and unfit for human consumption" and allegedly "possessed no health-giving properties over and above ordinary water." Shipments of the water

had been seized and condemned in a dozen cities. The record was clear. No one had even attempted to defend the water.

7.   The product was obviously in bad. The company owning the spring was in bad. If there was any doubt as to whether I was in bad, there will not be after I tell you that all the stockholders in my water company had previously bought stocks through me when I had been with an investment banking house and this latter outfit was now also in trouble.

8.   Those stocks, which up to then had regularly paid dividends, suddenly began to pass them. The investment company, itself, was being charged with fraud in connection with the sale of securities.

9.   I was holding a wildcat by the tail. Even if I could hold on, there seemed no point in doing so. Looking back, I can't tell you why I did not follow advice freely and unanimously offered by well-meaning friends to take my losses and get out. In my case, "getting out" meant out of town. I could not very well have lived down the series of losses inflicted on my relatives and best friends.

10.   It was probably well that I did not have a cent with which to move out of town. Then too, I had a wife and two boys.

11.   Whatever the reason, and I honestly don't know even now what it was, I held on. The immediate problems confronting me were how (a) to make our fifty year contract valid, (b) to establish the purity and therapeutic property of the mineral water we were to

sell, and (c) to satisfy my own stockholders who were calling for liquidation of the newly-formed company.

12. The matter of how to sell the water profitably to an uninformed and skeptical public seemed to me an inconsequential detail at the moment. My faith in the water's health-giving properties was strong. My enthusiasm was not at all dampened by my lack of business experience.

13. Upon reflection I find I owe much to my lack of experience. I was probably saved from disaster and pushed into the "successful" class by this very lack of experience. I would go further. I believe that had I followed the orthodox procedures of every one in my line, I'd have gone broke long ago. I've succeeded because I didn't know any better. Not knowing, I left much to my Partner. He always knew the answers. But I am running ahead of my story.

14. The three main problems confronting our water company were not really solved. We simply prevented them from annihilating us. I arranged with the owners of the spring to use some of the $50,000 we paid them to satisfy bondholders who had forced the company's receivership. We called upon the Food and Drug Administration and told them of our new bottling and sterilization equipment to insure the natural purity of the water, and also of our plan to restrict claims to those made by reputable physicians. We called a meeting of our stockholders and while all were dismayed at the turn of events only one demanded immediate liquidation of the company. I bought his stock by

giving him a third mortgage on my house.

15. We had just about exhausted our working capital. I interested a man with wealthy connections who agreed to put $30,000 into the company in exchange for control. After I had secured the unanimous approval of the deal by the stockholders, my wealthy friend backed down.

16. The deal he had drawn up, however, looked good to one of the stockholders—a man of strong gambling instincts—and he took it on.

17. We started to sell the water, but met with head-on opposition on the part of organized medicine. I should explain here the reasons for the difficulties we encountered for the next 27 years with the American Medical Association and through its influence with the Food and Drug Administration. This latter, a branch of the Government, is committed to protect the public from harmful food and drugs and from fraudulent claims, and has achieved a splendid reputation. For many years before and after the turn of the century, physicians in this country had been victims of unfair competition on the part of quacks with nostrums of all sorts. The American Medical Association, in an effort to give the physician the protection he deserves, decided to wage a vigorous fight against the existing vicious competition. Lumping into one package every commodity that did not call for a doctor's prescription or advice, the A. M. A. started a campaign to eliminate them from the market. In this group were included mineral waters, which were then quite popular in this

country, as were the spas from which the waters came.

Purveyors of these mineral waters were themselves somewhat to blame for their inclusion with patent medicines and nostrums, because they had been making ridiculous and unproved claims for the therapeutic qualities of the various waters.

It was quite natural for the Food and Drug Administration to accept a "directive" of this sort from the A. M. A.; even today they are guided by the consensus of medical men on any subject having to do with health. Obviously no one should be better qualified to pass on such matters than a physician.

18. In spite of obstacles sales grew, customers repeated and told their friends. A small number of physicians recommended the water to their patients. We tried a modest direct mail advertising campaign to attract new users.

19. The owners of the spring wanted more money from us and were insistent in their demands. Each day came a special delivery letter or telegram to my home or office. The wording of each was different but the threat was the same: "Send money or else." Finally their threat was made good. The water running into our bottling plant was shut off. The owners claimed we owed them more than a million dollars. Our contract called for payment of five cents per gallon for all water taken from the spring. As 200,000 gallons daily flowed through our plant, they demanded $10,000 a day. Actually we were only bottling 500 gallons or $25. worth a day. We went to court and secured a

mandatory injunction restraining the owners of the spring from interfering with the flow of water into our plant.

20.   For five years we progressed and declared our first dividend. Then without warning the Food and Drug Administration swooped down on our warehouse, seizing the water there on the charge that it was misbranded and polluted. The same charges had put other agencies out of business.

21.   The health authorities of the state in which we were selling the water were persuaded that our water was a source of danger to public health and that its sale should be instantly prohibited.

22.   Both Federal and State authorities jointly entered our warehouse on a liquor warrant (it was during Prohibition) and seized the water from a freight car that had just arrived. This move was calculated to destroy us, leaving us no water to sell.

23.   Immediately upon the first seizure we had taken samples of the water to five separate reputable chemists for analysis. They reported the water absolutely pure—several stating it was the purest water they ever analyzed, showing no bacteria at all.

24.   We learned that the State Health Laboratory had made the same finding: the water was pure and free from contamination. The State thereupon dropped from the case and we received a personal apology from the Secretary of Health.

25.   However, there had been introduced into the legislature of this State a bill that would prohibit

the distribution of any water "suspected" of being polluted. All that was needed under this Act was to *suspect* that our water was bad. No proof was necessary. A water company was required to get a permit to do business, and could not operate without it.

26.   When this bill was passed, the head of the State Health Department was importuned by the Federal authorities to refuse us a permit.

27.   When it appeared that a permit might be withheld from us, I called upon the head of the State Health Department and suggested that he make an investigation of the spring, even though located in another state. I voluntarily offered in writing to abide by the findings of his own experts. If their findings were against us we would go out of business.

28.   At my request he agreed to send two of his best men, the chief sanitary engineer and the chief chemist of the State Health Department to make a personal inspection of the spring and the surroundings.

29.   As a result of the findings of the State's experts, we were among the first granted a permit to sell our water in that State despite pressure from the Federal authorities.

30.   The next move came from the State in which our spring was located. Despite the fact that the spring had been state owned and operated for more than a hundred years, the State Health Department was persuaded that the spring was dangerously polluted. On these grounds, the Health Department sent out a notice to the Health Department of every state in the

Union urging that the sale of our water be prohibited.

31.   We went to court and produced evidence upon which the Judge issued a mandatory injunction requiring the State Health Department to withdraw the notices sent out to each state. This order of the Court has never yet been complied with.

32.   The trial in the U. S. District Court to determine whether the water seized by the Food & Drug Administration was impure and misbranded stretched out for four years. At the conclusion of the case the Judge ruled in our favor. He found the water free from pollution and misbranding.

33.   An appeal was taken to the Circuit Court of Appeals, which unanimously affirmed the decision of the District Court.

34.   We got word that an appeal was to be taken to the Supreme Court, but that Court did not hear the appeal. We had definitely won the case.

35.   In the meantime the great Depression hit the country. Along with other business, our sales slumped decidedly.

36.   About this time, the owner of the Spring who was still demanding additional money from us, tried a new angle. Most solicitously, he told us we were in danger of losing our bottling machinery. "The man holding a mortgage on the bottling plant building is going to foreclose and, under the state law, the machinery would be confiscated. You can prevent the foreclosure by raising $11,000," he told us.

37.   We learned that while this story was not true,

one with a greater threat to us was: the bondholders on the Spring were planning foreclosure action. This would make our contract worthless.

38. We arranged to meet with a group of the bondholders in a city 300 miles distant. They were a discouraged lot, having held the bonds for a dozen years without getting interest. The Depression was on, and Federal authorities had succeeded in putting every distributor of the water out of business except ourselves.

39. The bondholders, however, would give me no assurance that in the event they took over the Spring, we would be given a contract, permitting us to carry on.

40. I reported this to my stockholders and urged that money be advanced to buy out the bondholders. No one supported my proposition.

41. I thereupon proceeded personally to negotiate with the bondholders. After three years of negotiation, I was able to acquire a controlling interest in both bonds and mortgage. I spent very little cash, having little, but issued quite a few personal notes.

42. Now I moved to make our contract valid. This required getting a clear title, in other words foreclosure. We were met with the information that the state had a prior lien for back taxes in the sum of more than $10,000. We reached a settlement whereby the state would institute the foreclosure proceedings and we would come in as first lien holders.

43. The owners of the spring succeeded in blocking foreclosure action by obtaining five postponements after I had made long trips with my attorneys to

the state capital.

44.   The Judge finally ordered the properties sold at public auction. By this time I had exhausted myself financially and was greatly in debt. The terms of the sale called for one third cash. My only hope was that the size of my holdings—by then several hundred thousands—would discourage other buyers.

45.   In July of 1932 (about the Depression's lowest point) on the steps of the county court house, before a small and listless crowd, the auctioneer appointed by the receivers sold the properties. I purchased them virtually without opposition and at a price little above the taxes.

46.   I began at once to put into effect my plans for national distribution of the water. Soon I had distributors in about 25 cities.

47.   Because I thought it was the right thing to do and good business as well, I reduced the price of a 5 gallon bottle of the water from $3.25 to $1.25. On the basis of our increased sales and future prospects, I applied to the RFC for a loan, under the Act just passed providing for loans to small businesses.

48.   After a most thorough investigation lasting more than a year, the RFC approved a loan to us. The amount, $35,000; the collateral, a first mortgage on the spring and all the real estate. They required that full payment of the loan be made within three years. My confidence in the prospects of national distribution of the water was such that I agreed to these rather exacting terms.

49. When I went to sign the contract and get the money, the lawyer representing RFC made some caustic remark about my success in having unloaded an old abandoned summer resort on the Government for $35,000. Considering the thoroughness of the investigation, this charge coming from one entirely unfamiliar with the details startled me. I found myself refusing to sign and instead withdrew my application.

50. Lacking funds and without prospect of getting any, I decided on some drastic moves. First, we would cut our expenses to the limit. We would give up our plans to achieve volume at a low price. The question was how to get back to the $3.25 price, as we were losing money at the $1.25 price, despite sales that had multiplied five times. Eventually we hit on a plan which permitted us by gradual increases over a period of years to get back to our $3.25 price. This plan also put some quick cash in our hands.

51. All my time and thought was still on the distribution of the water. As for the physical property that had once been a summer resort, I had it in the back of my mind that some day some of the profits from the water business would go to putting one or two of the old buildings in shape.

52. My efforts to borrow money were fruitless until a former governor of the State, then president of a small bank in our county seat, agreed to lend me a small sum, as he said, "on my face."

53. We spent this money on one of the buildings. The place at one time had been one of the leading re-

sorts of the south, but had been abandoned for almost
a quarter of a century, following a fire that had razed
the principal building. The village nearby was poverty-
stricken. It consisted of a few shacks. The villagers
were so eager for work they were glad to take jobs
for a few cents an hour. We paid 50% over the pre-
vailing rate. Although it was during the Depression I
still feel sick at heart when I think of this low wage
rate. If, during our first season, we had more than eight
guests over a week-end, it was cause for rejoicing.
The second year the hotel business doubled and my
banking friend increased his loan to us. The third year
our hotel receipts tripled, and our bank credit was
slightly increased. The receipts, however, did not cover
the expenses of running the place and the necessary
repairs.

54.   Back of our main building was a plateau which
invited the construction of a golf course. A friend
volunteered to lay out a nine hole course, refusing
payment even for his expenses. Working with hand
labor and a brace of mules we built six holes in one
year and three more a few years later.

55.   All this time, I was desperately striving to put
over a big deal on the water. Between the years 1934
and 1939, I had dealings with six different parties, each
with strong financial connections, regarding plans for
national distribution of the water. In several instances
the chances seemed good that the deal would go
through. In each case I was prepared to agree to almost anything to clinch the deal.

56.   In each case I was to get a large sum of money, a good salary as manager and a good-sized interest in the business. In each case, something came up to block the deal. I just could not put one of these deals across.

57.   While the water business was at a standstill, the receipts from the resort were increasing. The fourth year was six times as good as the first.

58.   Along about this time the Federal Trade Commission took action against us on the charge that our water had no therapeutic properties over and above Potomac River water. At the hearing, the Commission produced three young physicians, all of whom testified they knew nothing about our water. Nor did they know any doctor who had had experience with it, nor any patient who had used it.

59.   Our witnesses consisted of five medical men of good standing and a chemist of national reputation. Each testified that he had no interest in our company nor was he being paid to testify. They had an average experience with the water of eleven years and testified that it unquestionably possessed therapeutic properties over and above ordinary water. They further stated, as their opinion, that any medical man not having had clinical experience with the water was not qualified to render an opinion as to its efficacy.

60.   The Examiner (appointed by the Commission), who had first looked upon us as frauds, was much impressed by the reputation and testimony of our witnesses. In a confidential opinion for the Commission

he urged that the case against us be dismissed.

61.   After an unusual delay of about a year, the Federal Trade Commission issued its findings, ordering us to cease and desist from claiming that our water "alone will cure" any ailment. No such claim had ever been made. Nor had we been charged with making it. It had not figured in the case. We went to the Court of Appeals, which took the Commission to task, but sustained the finding "only because of its limited nature." However, we could now say exactly everything we had said before, adding only "We do not claim or imply that our water alone will cure." At last we thought this issued settled. The case had extended over three years.

62.   In the meantime things at the resort kept growing. The year America entered the war, 1941, our receipts had increased 25 times over the first year.

63.   Our two boys went into the service. (By this time, we had added two girls to our family.) As ours was a family-operated place, the boys were missed, of course. Our problems in the war, however, were small compared to those of others. We wondered what traveling restrictions would do to us. We soon got the answer. Our rate of increase was accelerated. By 1942, our receipts were forty times greater than our first year.

64.   In June of 1943, there came an official communication from the Food and Drug Administration to the effect they were considering criminal action against me personally. The charge: I was fraudulently

asserting our water had therapeutic properties when it was no better than Washington tap water. I referred them to the Federal Trade case. The Commission had gone into this question most thoroughly. I added that if they had any suggestion as to what should be put on our labels, we would give it earnest consideration. Their response was to seize without warning all the water on hand in a New York City warehouse. This time there was no charge that the water was not pure—only that it had no health benefits.

65.   Realizing the hopelessness of matching financial resources with so powerful and persistent an adversary, I again offered to amend our labels so as to free them of any claim whatever. Under the new Food, Drug and Cosmetic Act, this offer could have been accepted and the case closed.

66.   The Food & Drug Administration refused the offer. We had no alternative but to fight the case even though the value of the water seized was only $35.00.

67.   This case has dragged out twelve years. As I write, word has just been received that the case was dismissed by the Court in our favor. This case has cost us more than 300 times the value of the water involved. Its effect on our water business was devastating; our sales in one city alone dropping from $65,000 annually to less than $8,000.

68.   I must now record an accident which at the time made all other matters seem unimportant. My

first-born, Porter, and his wife Ruth were returning to our resort from a city some 200 miles distant, when the car went out of control on the Pennsylvania Turnpike. In the head-on crash that occurred, Ruth was instantly killed and Porter severely injured. Early reports of his grave condition proved unfounded, and the fear of internal injuries and of damage to the brain were later dispelled.

69.   Things meanwhile at the summer resort had progressed almost fantastically. At the end of our tenth year, we were being booked a year ahead. At the end of our 15th season, we had grossed 100 times our first year. In our 20th year, the volume was 150 times our first year.

With the growth of the place came generous offers to purchase our property. Offers also were made to finance the construction of a large modern hotel. Because we have come to enjoy our work, we do not propose to sell or to change what is here. We will never get over the wonder of what has happened to us.

Picture it if you can. Suppose at the lowest point of the Depression a good friend comes to *you* for advice and tells you *this* story:

He has come into an old abandoned summer resort, hidden away in the mountains, thirty miles from the nearest town. The road leading to it is narrow, mountainous and in spots dangerous. The place is without utilities—neither electricity nor gas, nor telephone. There is no kitchen, dining room or living room, the main building having burned to the ground 22 years before. The few remaining buildings are of frame construction and badly in need of repairs; the furniture in them meager and obsolete, the beds hard and uncomfortable. There is no plumbing anywhere—one has to go outside for water, which comes from a mineral spring, health-giving and of generous supply. Your friend has no money, and because the Depression is on, he finds it tough to raise money.

He then says to you: "That's my situation. Now here's what I'm supposed to do with this place in a few years time, and I'm asking your advice how to go about doing it. I'm supposed to change this picture so that it will look like this: A beautiful and appealing summer resort, adequately caring for 200 people in about 100 fairly modern rooms, almost all with private bath; living rooms and dining rooms to meet the needs; two nine hole golf courses, one of regular size, the other a pitch and putt course, tennis courts, swimming pool, a private fishing pond, and also a 1000 foot frontage on a nearby river; all other forms of recreation found at a quality summer resort. I am to acquire and operate several farms where I am to raise all the necessary vegetables, fruits, and grains, several thousand turkeys, chicken and ducks, several hundred sheep and a greater number of hogs (from the latter I am to produce country smoked hams, bacon, sausage, etc.); thirty head of milk cattle, enough egg layers to supply fresh eggs daily for all the guests and workers; I am to have modern machinery to meet all our needs: tractors, bulldozers, trucks and mechanical farm equipment. My land holdings are to be increased from 320 acres to 5000. I am supposed to build a dozen new buildings, including a deep freeze plant alone worth $30,000."

Your friend pauses a moment, then says: "I've told you what I've come into and what I'm supposed to make of it. Now I'll tell you the rules under which I am supposed to operate. I am not to raise any capital. I am not to allow any mortgage or bond or other indebtedness to be placed against the property. Everything I acquire I must own outright. I must get a good road for the 30 mile stretch leading to the property. I am supposed to get the summer months booked a year ahead. And all this growth must be accomplished without advertising or publicity."

Your friend stops, this time as if he has told all. You know, however, that he hasn't told everything; he hasn't mentioned the greatest obstacle of all, and his failure to recognize it as a roadblock points up the acuteness of his problem. The thing your friend forgot to tell you was that he had no taste for the job he was supposed to do. He did not believe it could be done under the existing circumstances. His mind was on something else—on distributing the water, not on developing the hotel. He'll soon be wasting thousands of dollars on the wrong thing, and it will be years before he can be persuaded to apply his energies in the proper place.

You suspect this, but how can you tell it to your friend? You know that he lacks both the vision to see what is ahead and the patience to see it through. Yet he is expecting some kindly and encouraging advice from you. How can you honestly give it? You wonder how one so inept and inexperienced as to get himself tied up in a worthless contract with an outfit having several huge encumbrances on record against it could have wiggled out of the awful mess in the first place. And to have not only come out of it free, but to have had the property handed to him as if on a silver platter!

* * *

The friend I've asked you to conjure up as coming to you for advice is of course myself. And the thoughts expressed in the hypothetical interview are really those that came to me as I sat alone one lovely summer day gazing at the property which had just fallen into my custody. Still marvelling how it all had come about, I traced back in my mind the events leading up to this unbelievable twist of good fortune. As the story unfolded, the jig-saw puzzle came to view, humbling me thoroughly by the revelation that I really had not laid a single piece of the completed picture by myself. Recognition of this humiliating fact led to the great discovery which revolutionized my life. If you already have come upon this same discovery in your own life, you know the happiness and achievement that follow in its wake. You may find comfort and satisfaction in having your own faith affirmed by the experience told here.

The Story Behind the Story

As THE RECORD shows, some 23 years ago I was dead broke and about to lose my job. The record goes on to show that real estate considered worthless when it came into my possession is now valued at over a million dollars.

But the record does not show the story behind the story, the interesting and pertinent facts that are more important than the story itself. For instance, the record does not show that it was only when I abandoned my desire to accumulate money for my personal and family benefit that things began to gravitate my way. Nor does it show that 23 years ago I had as few *real* friends as has the average person and that today I love more people and in turn receive the affection of more than I ever dreamed possible.

Years ago my ambitions were fixed on achieving great financial success. Today I find myself bent on repaying the many kindnesses done me. My early notions about happiness had revolved almost entirely around my own ego. Now I know for a fact the only real happiness I will ever have must come from submerging my ego. When things went against me, I used to be depressed or demoralized. Now I believe all things are for the best.

What brought this change from failure to success—from drudgery and worry to radiant, joyous living? The answer is, I discovered I had a Partner. It was as simple as that.

I discovered that the Spirit which created me had not gone off and left me on my own. This Spirit had integrated itself with my being in an eternal Partnership. I began to find proof of this Partnership everywhere and in everything. I learned and I have had to relearn a thousand times since, that my place in the Partnership is not in the number one spot. I am the *junior* partner, taking orders and doing my appointed work. It goes wonderfully well—*so long as I keep myself out of my Partner's way.*

Everything that has happened to me since the great discovery almost a quarter of a century ago has strengthened my faith in the Partnership concept. After that day when in my mind's eye I saw the enlightening jig-saw puzzle all put together with not one piece of it laid by myself, I could no longer deny that a Power far greater than myself had been directing my fortunes. I had been the beneficiary of many things I could not have achieved alone, some of them done before I was born.

When I realized that I did not stand alone, I spoke my first words to my Partner: "I see your Hand in all this. And as You have planned to bring this property and this spring under my care, I promise I will not use my trusteeship to keep a lot of money for myself and family. Rather I will see that the water is made available to those who need its healing properties. And I will devote myself as much as possible to helping others understand the potential happiness that can be theirs through the Partnership You planned with each of your children."

The promise was made as if to another individual. It may have been only an oral contract. In fact, it may not even have been that, as my words were inaudible. But the words were in my heart and my Partner did not need an interpreter to understand them, nor I did not require a lawyer to hedge them about with technical loopholes.

Many times since then, of course, I have impatiently acted as if I knew better than He what should be done and how to do it. On these occasions I worked feverishly on plans for quick success. Some of these plans carried over a year or two. *But each time I met with defeat and frustration.* Later, when the picture cleared and I was able to see events in their true perspective, I realized that if I had been permitted to go on my own way, I would have lost my shirt. The deals which were calculated to make a lot of money would have brought me to ruin.

My Partner saw to it that I did not have my way. He knew that I was not ready for the success I was trying to get too soon. It was only after four of these "big deals" fell through over a six year period that two important conclusions forced themselves upon me.

The first was that the uses of adversity really *are* sweet. I benefited from each of these setbacks. The door had been closed to me, but for a purpose. Another door, leading to greater and truer happiness, was to open for me. As I look back now, it is crystal clear that every frustration and misfortune I have ever had has in some way reacted to my good. Disappointments do not long stay bitter with me now. I have learned that it is not given me to see the whole picture too soon.

The second conclusion I reached was to stop kidding myself that I was running the show. Only after I accepted the fact that my place was not in the driver's seat but in the helper's spot did I begin to be happy and get real results. The driver's seat was reserved for my Partner. He knew what the score was and also what the score was to be, this latter depending of course on the degree of my co-operation with Him. When I was content to be an instrument through which He worked, things really clicked. When I tried to take over in an effort to speed things along, I got in trouble.

I came upon the great discovery a few hours after the property had come my way. But I realize now there were many events that led up to the discovery.

When things began coming my way, I saw the hand of a Power greater than my own working in countless ways to help me. But at first I did not think of this Power as my Partner. I had never been a religious person. My parents were agnostics. I had never thought much about God one way or the other until the day of the great discovery. Then it came to me that God is a loving creative Spirit, not a stern figure a million miles off waiting to judge us after death, but

part of our very being here and now. I have reached
the positive conviction that the Creator made man to
live in Partnership with Him. I can find no other purpose to life.

When I got the green light from my Partner, everything came off according to plan, my Partner's plan.
I have really tried to live up to my end of the deal.
Moreover, I have told my children and hereby serve
notice on them and their children and all who enter
the family via marriage that part of this deal includes them. And that part is this: If I or my family
or their families at any time forget we are trustees
only, if we conduct ourselves as though the place were
our property and to be used for our own personal
gain, we will lose it. And in losing it we will have failed
our Partner, for the possibilities that are ours to help
people are beyond our vision.

* * *

After the agreement was made, I discovered that
my Partner had anticipated my making this offer to
him. He had been preparing for it for years. Authorities on love affairs say that the man only thinks he
does the proposing, when as a matter of fact the woman has so subtly handled matters as to bring about
the proposal. Likewise authorities on spiritual matters
say that it is not man, but God, who initiates an offer
of the type I made.

Let me cite some of the ways my Partner's hand
figured in my affairs, always working for my true

interest and happiness. He did not always give me what I wanted. Often that would have been the worst thing that could have happened to me. Many of His greatest favors were in the nature of hard refusals. Let us analyze the events as numbered in the story beginning on page 3.

* * *

1. "The time of the discovery was July 1932, about the very bottom of the Depression." The Depression caused a great drop in our sales, but it enabled me to pick up the bonds on the spring at the next-to-nothing price I paid for them.

* * *

2. Could anyone have paid out $50,000 to a man in receivership under the conditions I did and got away with it, unless he had "angels looking after him?" Any smart person, after learning the situation, would have taken his loss and got out. Someone was surely looking after a fellow who had not enough sense to look after himself. It is easy enough now from a hindsight position to say I should have stuck it out. But who could see it that way when the heat was on?

* * *

6, 17, 20, 21, 24-30. The Food and Drug Administration action on the purity and health-giving qualities of the water was of course troublesome, but it combined with the Depression to reduce the cost to me of the bonds at a time when I had not the funds otherwise to purchase them.

15, 16.   Had the man who promised to put in the $30,000 kept his agreement, I would shortly have been out of the picture altogether; for I learned later that he was the dictator type, one with whom I could never have worked for any length of time. But the deal this man had proposed and then backed down on was taken up by another man with whom I *could* work. He had confidence in me and I in him. Will someone explain why the desired deal went through, but not with the party I had approached?

* * *

19.   The attitude of the owners of the spring in hounding us for money and shutting off our water supply, while annoying and troublesome, was paving the way for the property to fall into our custody.

* * *

36-41.   My Partner's touch is evident in the whole history of the mortgage bonds; the willingness, almost eagerness, of the bondholders to unload them; my ability to purchase the bonds with personal notes and virtually no cash; the sale that took place at the Depression's low point. Too many things happened at propitious moments to call them chance. They were all part of a wonderfully conceived plan, in which my Partner demonstrated His power to salvage blessings from man's errors.

* * *

54.   My Partner helped me in many other ways: the building of the golf course, for example, without which

the resort's growth could never have been achieved. While I appreciated the need for a golf course, we would have let it ride because of lack of funds had not an amazing incident occurred. On the streets of a large city I met an old friend who introduced me to his companion. This fellow was a well-known amateur golfer who had long wanted to lay out a golf course. He offered to do it for us. On a cold bleak winter day he made the survey and brought back with him a sketch which was altered only very slightly in construction. What inspired this person, who could not stand long rides without getting sick, to make a 450 mile round trip to our place and to refuse to take a penny for his efforts, expenses or time? What induced him to follow through for me, find a golf architect, help get the necessary equipment and start work on the golf course at a time when everything was at rock bottom cost?

* * *

55.   When I first made the deal with my Partner, I was under the impression that what was expected of me was to see that people most needing the water would get it and be benefited. Assuming that this was my whole assignment, I gave no thought to doing anything with the resort. That it would shortly turn out to be the most profitable end of the business I could never have believed.

To rebuild at that time seemed out of the question. The grounds and buildings were in a frightful state of disrepair and an engineer's survey had shown that even at 1933 prices more than $100,000 would be required to get started. Even if we did rebuild, this still left us with bad roads and no electricity or telephone. Moreover, the place had been abandoned for almost a quarter century, and advertising should be needed to let people know it was once more a resort.

It seemed clear to me that the thing to do was to give the resort no serious thought at this time, but rather to devote myself to making the water business profitable. This course seemed entirely sensible and practicable. Even when the receipts from the resort multiplied in the first few years, I had not the vision to see what was soon to be. I spent almost all my time and thought on the water business. I was so conscious in those early days of the deficiencies of the place— hard beds, no bathrooms, no electricity or heat—and I was so unhappy about them, that I tried to turn the operation of the resort over to others. The last thing in the world for which I considered myself qualified was to run a place of this kind. I was an introvert by nature and self-conscious to a pitiful degree most of the time. I was uncomfortable with people and shuddered at the thought of meeting and mingling with them, particularly under the inadequate conditions then existing.

When I look back and realize how earnest and desperate were my efforts to get someone else to operate the resort for me, almost to the point where I was willing to give an outsider a good-sized interest in it to take the job off my hands, I marvel at the manner in which my Partner parried all these efforts and by one deft touch or another simply made it impossible for me to throw the place away.

At that time, these maneuvers looked like defeats and frustrations to me. I had neither the faith nor the vision to see ahead. My mind was intent on sticking to what I thought was expected of me: to get the water to those needing it. I have now learned that guidance is a flexible thing. Also that "Be still and know. ." means: "I am with you. Take it easy. Don't press. Keep yourself open for guidance all the time." I work best now when I say, "Keep thou my feet. I do not ask to see the distant scene. One step enough for me."

Most marvelous to me was my Partner's faith in me. He attributed to me a sincerity I finally dared not betray. The words of Dr. Carrel, the great surgeon and scientist, took on a new significance: "Even if we are pitifully dumb, or if our tongues are overlaid with vanity or deceit, our meager syllables of praise are acceptable to Him and He showers us with strengthening manifestations of His love." Certainly, this has worked out for me to a degree far beyond my understanding.

Here I am today, an almost complete failure in the thing I wanted most to do and at which for about 32 years I worked hardest to achieve. And on the other hand, the thing which at first was most distasteful to me and the amazing growth of which I could not envision at all, has become an unusually successful venture. It is a strange development—altogether too strange to be an accident.

Often I have searched far afield for answers to my problems, only to find them close at hand.

My determined efforts to get someone else to run the hotel end of our business during the first few years of our ownership would probably have continued had I not finally had my eyes opened. I discovered that my wife enjoyed meeting and mingling with the guests, and was doing much to make them feel at home. Where I was unhappy in my consciousness of the shortcomings of the place, she seemed able to close her mind to what couldn't be helped. By her smile and naturally friendly manner, she enabled the guests to forget what the place lacked. Her own spirit supplied something more precious than the things in short supply. How close had I come to forcing my way to grief! This happens every time I try to run the show, instead of letting my Partner handle it in His own good time.

Not once in those first few years did my wife interfere with my efforts to get someone else to manage the hotel. Hers was a much better way. By being her own sweet self, she opened my eyes to the realization that the "Acres of Diamonds" I was seeking elsewhere were in my own backyard.

That she is part of the Plan has since been proved in many ways. She is loved not only by the guests, but by all our co-workers too. Their own friendly attitude to the guests is a reflection of her attitude toward them. She treats the co-workers as the equals they are, and they respond. We have never had difficulties of any sort with our co-workers. Never has one asked us for a raise. It has been our practice to give increases each year as our business has grown. Bonuses are given regularly and each co-worker shares in the profits.

My wife's attitude is reflected in our children. They all love the place and love their work. This feeling has communicated itself to those who have entered the family by marriage. Anyone marrying into our family recognizes that he or she is marrying an institution; that for half the year at least, life is lived in a goldfish bowl. But our Partner's inspiration is evident in the love and harmony that pervades our family life and spills over into the lives of others.

Even more remarkable is the fact I, too, have grown to love my work. And the guests love us. In their kindness, they have given our family credit for the spirit of the place which they themselves have so largely created.

We are for the time being trustees for this beautiful and blessed spot, and are therefore in the picture, but it is our guests—now our warm friends—who have done the rest. We were not hotel people, and we approached this work back in 1933 in fear and uncertainty. Not knowing any better, we operated the resort as we would run our own home.

We know what this place was like when we took over more than two decades ago. And we know who brought about the change from a handful of guests to where our capacity is taxed a good deal of the time. This work was done for us by the kind words of kind

friends. Theirs was the major contribution to a
unique development: a Shangri-La, many have
called it, where hosts, guests, co-workers and com-
munity get along together in happiness and with
benefit to all.

* * *

The constant need of rehabilitating the buildings
and grounds required not only that all profits be put
back, but also that additional funds be borrowed from
banks. This proved to be another great blessing. It
protected our whole family from the danger of having
money to spend on ourselves. The children particularly
were conscious of the large debt that piled up before
each opening day, and personal expenditures by each
member of the family accordingly were kept to a
minimum. This was done simply because there was
no cash available to be spent. The result was a greater
appreciation on the part of the children of the limited
salaries they received. It saved us the unhappiness that
comes from spoiled children.

53.   I referred here to the people of the village nearby. We owe very much to these folk. Without them
we would have got nowhere. They gave us, and are
giving us today, the most loyal and conscientious co-
operation anyone could hope for. Over one hundred
of them work with us, and they are among our closest
friends and supporters. The shacks in the village have
disappeared and in their places are good sound houses.
They own cars and have bank accounts and are kind,
happy American citizens. I think that my Partner's

touch is evident in this wonderful set-up that was awaiting us in the village close by.

* * *

50.   There were many other ways in which we were looked after. If we had had money, we would have done what is considered the correct and orthodox thing to do when a summer resort seeks business: advertise. If the advertising had been successful it would have changed the whole character of our place. We would have been like a little country boy trying to look like a city slicker. Ours is a simple, unpretentious set-up, but with advertising we would have had to appear something we are not. Soon there might have been a rather stiff, formal atmosphere, with guests and possibly management as well vying with one another to put on airs and a false front.

Then there was also the chance that the advertising might not be successful soon enough, and this would have meant financial disaster. Being without means to advertise also did this for us: it drew our guests closer to us; in their kindness they did the advertising for us. Of course, later we were able to make "no advertising" our definite policy. But the foundation for that policy, which proved so important a factor in our success, was established by the necessity laid upon us by a Power greater than our own.

* * *

55-56.   My efforts toward rapid expansion and profits in the water business almost got me in *real* trouble.

I had approached the first two wealthy prospects myself. Other offers came unsolicited. In these cases I did not have much trouble persuading myself that an "angel" was being sent. And the idea of a short-cut to success certainly had its appeal. When after a year's negotiation the first deal fell through, I felt keen disappointment and a big let-down. I had the same reaction when the second deal went by the boards. But by the time the other deals failed, the picture had cleared enough for me to see my Partner's activity in the affair.

Sober reflection and critical analysis of these setbacks brought to light the fact that the net result was good for me. Eagerness to get ahead too fast almost cost me the heavy price usually paid for selling one's birthright. If any of these deals had gone through, my family and I would have had some money with which to feel comfortable for a time, but that would have been all. I shudder at the thought of what the rest of the picture would have been like. I am deeply grateful for each of those frustrations and for the forgiveness that overlooked my over-zealousness.

* * *

I am a practical person and cannot accept things on blind faith alone. There must be reasons. And the way I have come to have faith in my Partner is through the most practical kind of reasoning, based on demonstrations of His power and His desire for true happiness for His children.

I believe in my Partner because everything about

me, everything I can think of, everything I've experienced and can see now and ahead of me, makes it
impossible for me not to believe in Him. "All that I
can see teaches me to trust the Creator for that which
I can't see."

I am only one of the many children He has been
pleased to create and look after. One cannot view His
many acts of kindness and love, things with which no
mortal man had anything to do, without feeling humble and grateful.

To worry in the face of all His blessings would be
not to trust Him. To be fearful of the future after
the way He has looked after me in the past, would
be to let my ego with its narrow selfish viewpoint re-
place the sound judgment that is present when my
Partner is running the show.

* * *

63.   When our two boys went into the service, their
absence was felt not only by us, but by our guests.
But I never was able to bring myself to pray specially
for their safe return. Not that I was sure they would
return and in sound shape. I just felt that this matter
was up to my Partner. He knew the hazards of war;
He knew the whole story. I did ask Him that faith and
strength be given my boys to help them bear up under
any adversity that might come their way. Now that
the war is over and both boys and the lad my daughter married are safely returned, I keep asking my
Partner the same thing. I go even a little further. I

ask that whenever soft spots appear, whenever things are going too smoothly for their own good, they be given the necessary setbacks to keep them close to their creative Partner and their fellow-man. For too smooth going is not good going. In my case I found myself too apt to take blessings for granted, too inclined to take credit for things which my Partner was doing for me, too prone to become self-satisfied, and a little too ready to believe myself deserving of the nice things kind friends aimed our way.

* * *

66, 67.   The continued effort of the American Medical Association working through the Government to get something into the record against our water has not resulted in any great harm to us.

Viewed as part of the whole picture, this matter is seen to have served a good purpose. It brought to a definite decision the feeling that had been growing upon us for years: to withdraw the water from the commercial field. If this water really has the remarkable healing properties that more than thirty years of close contact convinces me it does in truth possess, then it should not be used for private profit.

The water is a gift from God. No man has anything to do in its preparation. It gushes up from deep in the earth, forcing its way through a huge sandstone formation in a steady stream that is uniform as to volume, temperature and ingredients regardless of weather conditions, drought or flood. Our part is to let this blessed handiwork of God run by gravity through sterile pipes into sterile bottles. Through The Partnership Foundation which was created some seven years ago for the purpose, this healing water is offered without charge to physicians, hospitals and worthy citizens. It is used to help people get well and keep them well. Particularly do we rejoice when the water is used to prolong the lives of citizens who are rendering a real service to their fellow-man. This phase of our work might never have developed if the distribution of the water had become a profitable operation.

Incidentally the water has proved of enormous benefit to the health of my family. We all have been free of the sicknesses that seem most common today: headaches, faulty elimination, colds, and more serious ailments like arthritis and rheumatism. I am confident that the water is at least partially responsible for this favorable condition, and this conviction has contributed much to my decision to remove the water from the commercial field and to extend its use as widely as possible to physicians, hospitals, and public-spirited citizens without charge or obligation.

A great American physician, George W. Crile, wrote: "The normal alkalinity of the blood is the keystone of the foundation of life." Perhaps it is because our mineral water is mildly alkaline that it has such great value to health. Now that the value of trace elements has been established, physicians again are looking into the lighter mineral waters. We want to co-operate with them, in the hope that the water will be used as much in a preventive as in a curative way.

When, after forty years of trying to go it alone, I first discovered I had a Partner, I was amazed at the many important things He had already prepared for our Partnership, while waiting for me to wake up to the truth.

2.   Take the case of how I made contact with the owner of the Spring. It was brought about through a man whom I had known only a few years, but who had become my best friend. If he had not been one of the kindest and most lovable of men, I would not have taken the first step—the colossal blunder of paying $50,000 for a contract not worth the paper it was written on.

You see, my friend was not a shrewd judge of character; he loved and trusted everyone. This trait occasionally got him associated with people whose motives were not as unselfish as his own. His confidence in the owner of the Spring first was in large measure responsible for my entering into the contract without investigating the title to it. Obviously had I investigated I never would have touched the proposition, for I learned (too late to do anything about it) that the Spring and property were mortgaged or otherwise tied up to the extent of six million dollars.

Yet this great blunder turned out to be a stepping stone to all the amazing good that followed.

Reflect also on how I happened to meet my kind-hearted and trusting friend, whose secretary I later became. I had passed a Civil Service examination as stenographer and headed the list. There was an opening

in a certain department of the city's service and the first
four on the list were sent for to be interviewed. The
head of the particular department left to his assistant
the matter of the selection of the stenographer. This
assistant picked someone other than myself. Before
the selected party could be sworn in, however, someone in the Department suggested that the four top men
be given a test. As a result of this test, I was given the
job. I became department stenographer, then personal
stenographer to the head, then assistant secretary and
finally secretary. The head of the department became
my best friend. It was through him that I met the
owner of the spring. Any break in the chain and this
story would never have been told.

The "self-made" man may say: "Well, that's just a
case of the better man winning out. He was the *best*
stenographer, so he got the job."

Well, let me tell you how I got to be the "best" stenographer. Before I took the course of stenography and
typing at high school, I had also taken these subjects
at business college during the summer. This gave me
the jump on the rest of the class. Why did I take the
summer course? I had to, in order to go to high school.
You see, I was raised in an orphan home with about
135 other children. All the children were sent out of the
institution after grammar school. I was the only one
sent to high school.

Was that because I was an exceptional student? No,
I was an ordinary student. I had broken my arm when
I was nine. It never had been properly set and an op-

eration had failed to help it. I was physically small and handicapped, and so I was made an exception and sent to high school. Earlier it had been arranged for me to work during off hours. That was why I was sent to stenography and typing class during the summer months, and that in turn was why I was good enough to pass first on the list and get the job.

Why was I in the institution in the first place? My father had died when I was five, leaving my mother and four children penniless. Was this a tough break for me? Far from it. While tragic at the time, like every other seeming misfortune, this was a blessing in disguise.

* * *

It is my earnest belief that our Partner has a separate pattern for each of His children, as individual as each snow flake and tree leaf. We need only to follow His guidance, and the pattern of our life will burst forth with radiant joyousness.

You may remember as a child making a drawing by connecting scattered numerals. You would begin with number one, draw a line to number two, thence to three and so on to the last number. By the simple act of letting your pencil follow the numbers in their proper sequence, you found that you had created something, maybe a man, maybe an animal, maybe a house. Whatever it was, you felt that you had created it. Of course all you did was to fill in a pattern that had been outlined for you. If you disregarded the order of things and skipped from number one to let us say 12 or 20 or any other number looking for a shortcut, you came out with no completed pattern, but a jumbled mess. It was only after I stopped looking for shortcuts and was content to be guided by a Higher Power that the pattern my Creative Partner had planned for me came into shape. It was quite a blow to my ego when I learned I was not the creator but only the instrument through which the thing was done. But now I find the satisfaction that comes from being an instrument for this Higher Power is immeasurably greater than any my ego could yield me. As an ego-driven man, I had not been representing myself but misrepresenting myself. My ardent desire to be something of myself had blinded my intellect and weakened my will. My recovery came from learning to obey the will of the Creative Spirit within.

Emerson wrote: "A little consideration of what takes place around us every day would show us that a higher law than that of our will regulates events; that our painful labors are unnecessary and fruitless; that only in our easy, simple, spontaneous action are we strong, and by contenting ourselves with obedience we become divine. Belief and love—a believing love—will relieve us of a vast load of care. O, my brothers, God exists. There is a soul at the center of nature and over the will of every man, so that none of us can wrong the universe. It has so infused its strong enchantment into nature that we prosper when we accept its advice. . . . The whole course of things goes to teach us faith. We need only obey. There is guidance for each of us,

and by lowly listening we shall hear the right word. . .
Place yourself in the middle of the stream of power
and wisdom which animates all whom it floats, and
you are without effort impelled to truth, to right and
a perfect contentment. . . Fear (revere) God and where
you go, men shall think they walk in hallowed cathe-
drals. . . The purpose of life seems to be to acquaint a
man with himself. *The highest revelation is that God
is in every man."*

* * *

I am leaving unmentioned countless incidents, some
major, some minor, each perhaps insignificant in itself, but together forming part of the jigsaw puzzle
that destined me to happiness. Each of these incidents
was beyond my own doing. Had any one of them not
occurred, the chain could have been broken. They all
had to happen, even though I fought some of them, to
bring about the good that has come to me.

I wonder if any man who has given thought to the
factors that have entered into his life can fail to give
credit to his Partner. Is someone asking "How about
the many men who are recognized 'successes' and who
sincerely believe they are 'self-made'?" Assuming that
what is meant are the money-successes, or those achieving fame or high position, I venture a guess that they
have not searched thoroughly enough behind the scenes
to get the facts.

Am I inferring that these men did not work hard,
didn't have vision and courage? Far from it. These
men may be credited with all of these things, but so

too may millions of others who did not meet with "success."

Why then are only a few "successful" while the many are not? I suspect it might be that our creative Partner hopes for greater things from the "successful" ones.

Maltbie Babcock's lines help me keep straight the part my Partner plays in my affairs:

"Back of the loaf is the snowy flour
And back of the flour the mill;
And back of the mill is the wheat and the shower,
And the sun and the Father's will."

* * *

Prosperity and blessings have been showered upon our place and our family. I am not speaking of material prosperity. As a matter of fact, the offers to purchase our property were not based on our profits. We operate on none too comfortable a margin to be attractive to promoters. Their offers were based on the profit possibilities if our place was run on a "business" basis and if sale of the water was aggressively pushed. Our wealth is in our relationships—those with our co-workers, our neighbors and our guests. Along with this, is the good will that inspires guests to book reservations a year ahead, and supplies a waiting list of people who want to visit us. Far above the material prosperity and the good will that is a part of it is the great joy that stems from the friendliness and affection shown us by the several thousand folk who come to our place each year.

How does one know real friends? By the way they come to your aid when you are in distress, for one thing. Such an occasion did come to us, and I tell it here because it proved as no other circumstance could the depth and sincerity of the feeling our guests have for my family.

68.   The accident happened on my 60th birthday. It had been a lovely day, and the guests had joined my family in celebrating the occasion. But I was alone when I got the news. The sun had just dropped behind the mountain, and the colorings were radiantly beautiful. Coming up the hill, I saw Ted. He is my second-born, a sensitive idealist soon to reach his thirtieth year. A glance at his face told me that tragedy had hit close to us.

He started to say "I've got bad news, Dad. . ." I interrupted him to ask "How bad?" His face was white and he struggled to keep the shock from me. "Plenty bad. Porter and Ruth were in an automobile accident." Porter is my first-born and Ruth was his wife. They were parents of two lads, one four years, the other sixteen months of age. "How bad?" I repeated. "Ruth was killed," he said. "My God!" escaped from my lips. "And Porter?" Ted was suffering as he said: "In a very unsatisfactory condition." I asked: "Where is he?" He replied: "In the Harrisburg Hospital. It happened on the Turnpike." I turned and left him. I had to be alone with my Partner.

How does one know he has a Partner? By the way He comes to your aid when in distress, for one thing.

He is the greatest friend you have. Now I walked alone, trying desperately to practice a simple routine which in the past always had brought me closer to God. (I will tell you more about this practice later. It combines the physical, mental and spiritual sides of life, and I consider it the greatest discovery of my life, excepting only the discovery that I had a Partner.) In a few minutes I felt able to go down the hill to see if I could comfort my family.

It was at this point that I first realized how deeply our friends really cared for us. All the guests who had heard the shocking news had gathered around my family and had taken them in their arms. Such an expression of genuine love and sympathy I had never been privileged to see before. It was as if each of these comforting people had suffered a personal tragedy. It was no longer our own immediate family that was grief-stricken. These good folks actually shared our anguish, and by that much they lessened our sorrow.

Porter and Ruth were returning from a three day trip when the accident occurred. They had gone to the city, two hundred miles distant, to purchase a winter home. They had spent the better part of the next day and night moving their furniture and arranging it. The next day they planned to return to our mountain place in time to help celebrate my birthday.

On the Turnpike Porter felt himself getting drowsy, so he turned the wheel over to Ruth. We don't know quite how it happened, because Porter at the time of the accident was asleep—the one thing, physicians told us later, that saved him from death. Somehow the car went out of control, crossed the median strip and crashed head-on into a car coming the other way, killing a woman and seriously injuring three others in that vehicle. Ruth was instantly killed and Porter, who was thrown out of the car, suffered fractures from his right cheek to his knee. Fortunately the early hospital reports of internal injuries and brain disturbances later were not confirmed. His recovery now is almost complete, marred only by a slight limp. The morning after the accident my Partner sent me help from an unexpected source. I was still struggling to keep His presence with me when I found a little hand in mine. It was that of my four year old grandson Steve, who had been made motherless only the day before.

"Grandpa," he said, "Mama's gone to heaven, hasn't she?"

"Yes," I replied.

Then a slight pause.

"When I grow up and get big, some day I'll go to heaven, won't I?"

"Yes, you will," I answered. "Then," said Steve, with assurance, "I'll see Mama."

And there it was. Steve had resolved his problem. Life on earth was but an interlude. He would join his mother some day. Steve had no idea that he had been sent that morning to comfort me. Our Partner works in all ways to help us. We need but get ourselves out of His way, and listen to His voice. I heard it that day in the words of a four year old child.

How does one really know that the Partnership Life works? By checking the results when it is tried against when it is not tried. All my unhappy, frustrated moments have come from trying to operate on my own. When my little self is at work, the result is never good. When I am able to get myself out of the way and let my Partner work through me, the radiations of love going out and coming back are thrilling beyond words, and the effects are helpful to all concerned. Try this out often enough, and you must come to the conclusion that the real purpose of life is to discover and work your Partnership.

Probably no greater returns have come to us than in the close ties of friendship that have grown between our guests and our family. Business and professional men, judges, newsmen, government officials and workers have told us how much this simple, unpretentious spot has done for them. The following note from W. M. Kiplinger, whose Kiplinger Washington Letter is favorably known to business men throughout the country, illustrates this: "I see the spirit is still there, the something that makes————Springs not just a resort or just a business. I hate to speak of service to mankind, for the term is much abused and prostituted, but I kinda mean something like that. You've got it. Go ahead and blush. . ." Of course we glow at this, for it is added proof that the Partnership Life works. We know, too, that what people find here they have brought with them. Our place just gives them the chance to let it come out. They feel free to talk about things that city life with its emphasis on materialism makes almost forbidden. They do not talk "religion," they do not say they see my Partner's hand in the operation of our place, but they know something is working here even if they can't find words for it.

These friends, sometimes hesitatingly, sometimes forthrightly, ask what our secret is. What is it that permits them to feel like close friends to other guests who a day or two previous were strangers?

The secret is simple: We are trying to let our Partner run the place. As long as we continue to do this, His spirit will permeate the very atmosphere. When we forget it and think we are pretty good on our own, the secret will be lost.

Does that sound like too simple an explanation? Nevertheless it is the true one. Fontenelle said: "If the Deity should lay bare to the eyes of men the secret system of Nature, the causes by which all the astronomic results are affected, and they finding no magic, no mystic numbers, no fatalities, but the greatest simplicity, I am persuaded they would not be able to suppress a feeling of mortification, and would exclaim, with disappointment, 'Is that all'?"

How sure am I that the Partnership Life works? I am probably most sure on those occasions when in thoughtless haste and impatience I take over control from my Partner who freely lets me follow my will. Quickly then I lose the wisdom and the heart-warming joy that is mine when He is in control.

Soon I am sufficiently humbled to crawl out of the

seat reserved for my Partner and ask Him to drive
who knows the way. In running the resort as in the
conduct of my personal life, it is the same—all goes
well so long as the Power greater than myself is in
command.

* * *

Some enterprising promoters have said to us rather
pityingly: "You people are asleep. You don't know
what you have. This could be the greatest resort in the
country." (Later we had the gratification of hearing
Edward R. Murrow, in a national broadcast, refer to
it without mentioning it by name as "one of the world's
most unique inns—never publicized.") Actually, of
course, it would be unthinkable to trade for money what
has been built here by my Partner and the friends He
sent to help us. We already have happiness in a most
unusual degree. Shall we sell it to buy money? This
view is related also to our decision not to expand further. An enlarged operation would take from us the
joy of personal contact with warm friends. A bigger
guest list would deny us the opportunity of spending
time with those whom we have grown to love.

We believe the secret of living—man's partnership
with God—has been made known to us. We believe
that each human being carries that secret with him, and
that he needs only to be made aware of it to understand
it and make it work for him. It is in this hope and belief that we have been impelled to reveal in these pages
details that we have hitherto deemed too personal to
tell even our closest friends.

This book is written because the simple but amazing truth revealed to me some twenty years ago—the truth which transformed my life and brought me happiness, friends, and peace of mind—could no longer be kept secret. I came upon this understanding through my own experience in the workaday world. I later found confirmation of it in the words and works of Christ, who taught that no man walks alone, that his Maker is integrated with each human being in a living, working partnership.

Clearly, the Partnership concept is not new in any sense. It is an old truth well known to man. I have dusted it off and presented it here in the simple context of my own experience.

I started this job some twenty years ago. I am a business man, not a writer, and setting down my experiences, particularly those of a personal nature, did not come easy. There were times without end when I felt frustrated. In a materialistic world, the demands of security pressed unceasingly upon me. When time and conditions permitted, no inspiration was forthcoming. Inwardly I complained. I was trying to render some service to my fellow man, and God was not cooperating with me. Now, in shame, I realize I should have asked myself: "Do you resent growing? Are you trying to say you've reached the point of complete readiness and God doesn't know it? Fool! Rest assured that when you are ripe, the time will be ripe, and all other things having to do with the particular situation will be ripe. Do you then consent with all your heart to the delay and give thanks you are still to grow." If there has been growth since, it has been in my unshakable faith in the truth and practicality of the Partnership Life of man and Maker. Events of the past two years have so shaped themselves as to compel the finishing of this work. It was as if a directive had been given me: "You've been at this long enough. Now get it out."

Life's Greatest Discovery:
God is Within You

ONE THING MY Partner made unmistakably clear to me: "Do not think that what has been done for you is for you personally. I do the same for anyone, given the opportunity. Do not keep the great discovery to yourself. Pass the truth along so that others may benefit as you have benefited."

By this time I was deeply aware that I had been blessed. I also knew that I was being rebuked. My Partner had counted on my being able to see for myself the simple truths He eventually spelled out for me. I should have known, without its being forced upon me, that I could not stand alone. I should have been able to detect the subtle hold ego had upon me, blinding me to the Higher Power within me. The rebuke was gentle but unmistakable and at times quite stern.

The important thing I learned in the beginning was that my Partner could speak to me, if only I got quiet enough to listen. Years later I came across the Biblical promise: "Behold I stand at the door and knock. If any man hears my voice and opens the door, I will come into him. . . "

I now firmly believe that God stands at the door of each of us, knocking. I must have been particularly hard to get to, because often my Partner had to knock so loud as to arouse me from a sound sleep. I would then lie still to catch what He wanted to tell me.

Thus I got into the habit of starting off each day with a "quiet time" with my Partner. During these periods (which are not limited to morning hours) I have learned that it is unnecessary for me to speak my thoughts. My Partner knows them before I can advance them. I am able therefore to concentrate on what He wants to get across to me.

The impact of these messages on my life has been so great that when they start coming, I hasten to jot them down, lest they be lost to me. Because these thoughts often come in the early hours of the morning, I find it advisable to keep pencil and paper by my bedside. His voice comes through clearest in the still hours, and I have had to learn to write in the dark, sometimes experiencing difficulty later in making out my scribbling.

How do I distinguish between my Partner's thoughts and my own? By this simple rule: If the thought is free from any "self" motive, I take it that it comes from my Partner. If, on close examination, the thought is found to be tied to some personal desire, perhaps one that I've tried to hide from myself, I discard it as not my Partner's thought but my own. This method has worked for me. It falls into the pattern of life's great decision: ego or God.

I have learned that all matters discussed between my Partner and me are subject to His further guidance.

The thought of today is subject to amendment tomorrow. "Keep Thou my feet, one step enough for me."
It should be emphasized that these "conversations" were really only thoughts flowing through me. They are not advanced (God forbid!) as God's words. I am sure you know what I am trying to say. You have had moments when inspiring thoughts came to you. You knew you didn't think them up; they came *through* you. Brother Lawrence, the layman whose "Practice of the Presence of God" is a classic, wrote: "Everyone is capable of such familiar conversation with God, some more, some less." Lincoln put it: "Whenever God wants me to do or not to do a certain thing, He finds a way to tell it to me." Lincoln explained one such occurrence: "It was as though written out by pen and handed to me. Hereafter thank your Heavenly Father, not me, for this." In those too seldom moments when I was able to get myself out of the picture, these waves of God would flow into me, conferring a sense of quiet strength and peace; these were indeed inspired moments. The conviction forced itself upon me that when man invites God to take over his mind, his Partner will inhabit, lead and speak through it. For the time being, man lives with a divine unity, God guiding, man doing. Man is wiser than he knows. If he sincerely wants to know how he stands in God, the correct answer will flow through him. That communication is an influx of God's mind into man's mind, every moment of which is memorable. God's light shines through us, His wisdom breathes through our intellect, giving us

ordinary people an understanding denied to wise men
who would be brilliant of themselves.

If you believe in prayer, you believe you can speak
to God. Would you deny that God could speak to
you? What does "Be still and know that I am God"
mean if not that God will speak to us if we become
quiet?

God also has a way, it seems to me, of directing
us to read the inspiring thoughts He has sent through
other men and women. I owe much to my Partner's
guidance in pointing me to the comforting and uplift-
ing words of Lincoln, Franklin, Emerson and others,
but above all to the words and works of Christ. Because I sincerely believe it was God's guidance that
led me to reading their words, I have not hesitated to
state it as such.

* * *

With few exceptions—and these are noted—all that
follows in this chapter (The Truth) are thoughts that
I believe came from my Partner. Even when they were
in the nature of stern rebukes, they were never without the warm, heartening assurance of His presence
and His desire to help.

You Are Greater Than You Know

(The rebukes which seemed to come from my Part-
ner—some gentle, some not so gentle—ran like this:)

I created life to be a natural turning toward happiness, as children naturally turn to play. I planned that you should live a full, rich life, in vigorous health, at peace with yourself and your fellow-man. I created within every human being an unlimited capacity for joy, achievement, love and peace of mind. This capacity is born of my own creative Spirit, the Spirit that created man and created the universe and sustains both. You, like every other human being, are part of that Spirit.

You do not, therefore, stand alone. You are not the individual you may suppose yourself to be. You are a Partnership, made up of (1) your visible self, and (2) an invisible Spirit which is one with the Spirit of your Maker. Some men call this a religious concept. It is more. It is the whole reason for man's existence.

What does partnership mean? A definition of partnership is "union in business." In a successful partnership, the partners work in mutual trust and confidence. Marriage is a higher form of partnership. A successful marriage results when two fit their lives together.

The highest form of partnership is the union of man

and Maker. Until man finds this partnership and endeavors to live as one with the creative Spirit, he "begins at no beginning and works to no end." The highest revelation that can come to you is that God is your ever-present active Partner. Aristotle said: "The realization of the Divine in man constitutes the most absolute and all-sufficient happiness."

One of the reasons many men in their mid-forties and early fifties are breaking down today is that they are trying to stand alone. When a man knows the truth of Lincoln's statement, "God is the silent partner of all great enterprises," he is free of the pressure, tension and strain that cause breakdowns, ulcers and coronaries.

* * *

Call me what you wish: God, Creator, Father, the Christ Spirit, Evolution, the Angel of Your Better Nature, the Forces of Nature—you know what is meant. The important thing for you to know is that I AM, that My Spirit is within you, integrated with your very being. I am, in truth, your ever-present working Partner. It is a simple, provable fact that you depend constantly and unceasingly on my Creative Spirit to maintain the life I have given you. It is true also that I depend upon you to carry out My plan of life: the unity of man and Maker. It is a perfect partnership plan.

What Are You?

Wʜᴀᴛ ᴀʀᴇ ʏᴏᴜ? When people look at you, they see a physical body. What they cannot see even with the most powerful microscope is that very important thing known as your mind, with which you think and give orders to your body. And of course they cannot see the things that go through your mind: your thoughts, your desires, your fears. So you are made up of a physical body that can be seen and a mind that cannot be seen. Your visible body takes orders from your invisible mind. Your mind says: "Let's walk." Your body gets up and walks. Your mind says: "Let's eat." Your body obeys. Hands put food in mouth, teeth chew, throat swallows, and that's that.

But hold on. Is that that? How about the work yet to be done? Who takes up where you leave off? By whose will is the food you have eaten transformed into blood, bone, muscle, brain? You would not claim it was your will. There is a limit to what your will and your mind can do. Whose will is it? Would you not say it was the will of a Power greater than your own?

Some folks explain to their satisfaction that this sort of thing just happens. "Body chemistry, you know." But the fact remains that there is operating within you a Will that is beyond your reach, a Will that is infinitely greater and more powerful than your will. This powerful Will is looking after your interests. It works for your good. It is your benefactor in all ways and all the time. If this Will were not present within you, and you had to depend on your own will to do the many vitally necessary jobs to keep you going, how would you go about it? How, for instance, would you go about changing meat and fruit and vegetables and milk and bread into things like flesh and skin and bone and other more vitally needed body replacements?

Tonight when you are ready for sleep, ask yourself: "During my sleep, in obedience to whose will do my lungs breathe in the air without which I would quickly die?" Here is another question: "Whose will keeps my heart beating?" Over 100,000 times each day, the heart pumps blood to all parts of my body. It is pumping minute after minute, twenty-four hours a day, year after year. Can you really dispute that there is operating within you every second of your life a Will that is greater than your own?

Only a supreme egotism would try to deny this obvious fact. Some men make excuses to get around admitting that they have to depend on a Power other than their own. This admission would hurt their pride. They have persuaded themselves they are "self-made," "self-sustained".

I gave man the ability to think and analyze. Is it too much to expect that man would understand the tremendous significance of this Power within him—that he would recognize it as the same Power that gave him life—that it is visible all about him? Dumb animals are guided by this greater Will within them, but egotistical man prefers to be guided by his own will. When you wonder why there is so much misery in the world, ask yourself whose will are men obeying, their own or Mine?

* * *

Your will desires above all else to survive, to live. Many allowances are made for the instinct of self-preservation. But while your human will is using this instinct as an excuse for selfishness and acquisitiveness, My creative Will is busily engaged in the actual work of preserving your life. Everything about you offers evidence that I intended your will and Mine to work together, to produce your highest happiness. But your will often is so bent on having its own way that My creative Will is left only to do the things necessary to insure your survival. It is My Will, not yours, that sends billions of blood vessels throughout your body, carrying needed nourishment to every part of your system and taking away poisonous waste. While My creative Will is thus devoting itself to your interest, your own will may be having fun or enjoying a good night's rest. It is My Will, not yours, that sees that your brain is supplied with the necessary elements so that you can think straight and carry out your plans.

Why do I work ceaselessly to keep your body and mind active and vigorous? Is it not because, having *put* you here, I want to *keep* you here, want to keep you *well* and *vigorous?* You were put here for a purpose.

To enable you to achieve that purpose, I made my
Spirit a living part of you. No other human being can
achieve the special purpose for which you were made
and for which you are now here.

You were selected out of billions. But as great an
honor as this is, you cannot rest on it. There is a definite part in life that you must take. "Many are called
but few are chosen." The chosen ones are those who
want more than anything else to fulfill the purpose for
which they were made. The others pass on without
really knowing what life is all about.

To go through life disregarding the presence of the
spiritual Power within you is to be like a man who
lives and dies in poverty, unaware that a priceless estate awaits his claim.

All your troubles spring from ignoring, knowingly
or unknowingly, my Presence within you. Your physical and mental ailments are almost always the result
of failure to observe my simple natural laws for body
and mind.

* * *

This is not to say that you are to sit back and wait
for your Partner to do everything. I need you as you
need me. But your place is as junior partner, not as
master. When you accept your Partner's guidance and
inspiration, you do far more and better work than
when you are under the delusion of working alone. In
your every thought and deed, you need the co-operation of a Will greater than your own. It is a question
of whose will rules. In its simplest terms, life asks:

"Who is your boss, ego or God?"

Does "Thy will, not mine" seem like surrendering to Me the free will I have given you? Its effect is to give you *greater* freedom, plus greater power, joy and peace of mind. Your troubles arise when ego takes over. The dark spot in your sunshine is but the shadow of yourself.

* * *

Let's go back to your beginning. You have just been born, and we are looking this new infant over. You are sweet, innocent and lovable. The world into which you were born was created in law and order. Man, by persistently violating his Creator's laws, has brought about a state of disorder. People older and supposedly wiser than you would have you believe that your coming on earth was an accident, and that all life is happenstance. Great scientists, however, know there is a plan to life. And where there is a plan, there must be a planner.

Your coming on earth was planned. You are a *planned* person. The Great Planner put you here. Moreover, to put you here, odds of billions to one against you had to be overcome. Overcoming such odds is nothing short of a miracle. Yet your Maker did this easily and simply. You rank with the greatest miracles of all time. This is neither jest nor flattery. It is plain truth.

The facts about this miracle are known to every physician. When people reflect upon these facts, they will gaze upon this new-born infant with enormous interest and respect. When one is chosen above a billion others, it is cause for wonderment. Yet that is what happened to you. And if it had not happened, you never would have been born.

At the time you were conceived, approximately 250,-000,000 sperm cells entered your mother's womb. Only one of these cells had your name on it. The other 249,999,999 did not. The chances of that particular cell coming through were less than one in 250 million. The cell with your name on it united with a certain cell (one of 10,000 or more) on your mother's side, and this resulted in you. Two other cells might have united, and thus a child might have been born, but that child would not have been you, any more than your brothers or sisters are you.

You had to be born at that particular time to be what you are. Any two other united cells would have brought forth a different person, with a different personality. The cell with your name on it would have passed on to regions unknown. That is what happened to the other life cells. It did not happen to you.

You came through. You were destined to come through when you did, where you did, and of whom you did. Your Maker brushed aside the billions-to-one odds against you in order that you might be born. Why?

Was it "just luck," just happenstance? In order to believe that, you must believe that the whole universe is a matter of happenstance. That the sun's rising each morning at its appointed time is accidental; that its location and control with relation to the earth, so perfect that a change of one degree on the average for one year would result in your burning to a crisp or freezing to death, is a matter of luck. That the sun's power to give you light and heat from a distance of 93 million miles is just a good break. That these and the millions of other things you have come to take for granted, are matters of luck and chance.

Could anyone persuade you that the products of your factory or kitchen are the result of happenstance, that you neither planned nor made them? So you, too, were planned and brought about. You came through because it was your Maker's desire. You were meant to be born—you—not one of the billions of others that could have been born. Why?

Because your Maker intends you to make some contribution to His Plan. What else could have prompted your selection? Epictetus said: "You came into this world not because you chose to—or where you chose to —but because the world has need of you." You are here for a purpose. There is not a duplicate of you in the whole wide world; there never has been; there never will be. You were brought here now to fill a certain need. Take time to think that over.

Relax a little from the pressure of things about you, things which when viewed in proper perspective are seen to be trifling and fleeting. Relax, and ask yourself: Why did I, your Maker, bring you through at this time? What is expected of you? Something great as the world looks upon greatness? Not necessarily. Not many can hope to become a Beethoven and say with him: "It is the acme of bliss to approach the throne of Deity and thence to diffuse its rays among mankind."

Your contribution may seem a very little thing. Some may smile at it. But remember the story of the juggler in a cathedral who could think of no other way to show his love for Me than to do his juggling act before the altar. Some scorned his performance and others were shocked by it, but the juggler's whole heart was in it. His was a work of complete adoration, and therefore he inspired others and brought them closer to their God.

I am not so much concerned with the "greatness" of your task as with the love with which the task is done. Quite conceivably you might pass from this earth not knowing the particular thing or things for which I brought you here. Ponder these words of Emerson: "The great man knew not that he was great. . . What he did, he did because he must; it was the most natural thing in the world, and grew out of the circumstances of the moment."

It may be that you are here to do something quite different from anything you now have in mind. If your heart is right, if it is your sincere desire to be a channel for your Partner, before your time comes to go, you will have done what you were made for. Just remember there *is* a Plan and there *is* a Planner. I planned you and I need you.

Let's take another look at you as a new-born infant. This helpless little thing is obviously not self-

made or self-reliant. He does not take credit for being
born or being born well, with physical and mental
faculties intact, or for the privilege of being born in
free America, or for the other blessings with which
he has been endowed. These clearly are gifts from his
Creator.

Yet this utterly helpless infant may some day come
to believe himself so strong as to have no need for
God as his Partner. He will have been persuaded that
he is superior to others and therefore entitled to more
of the world's goods than his brothers. He will believe
that life is a race to get things, and he will set out
to get all the things he can. He will feel that the race
of life is to the swift and that he is among the swift.
As for talk of a Power greater than man's, he will
not be able to see how God could possibly interest Himself in all the billions of human beings on earth. Imag-
ine this creature of mine limiting God's capacity to his
own! He will believe that he stands alone and that in his
own little dynasty he is king. This is what happened to
you. You thought you were an individual, a "rugged
individual" going it alone.

Like many others, you were the victim of a situation over which you had no control. Much of your
training—at home and at school—led you to believe
you were on your own, and that I, your Maker, was
in some distant heaven, waiting to sit in judgment
on you.

But now you must understand the truth. There can
be no such thing as a "rugged individual" for the

simple reason there is no such thing as an individual. Each person is in individual partnership with me. I have integrated my Spirit within each human being, making of him a Partnership, he and I working together. Let your mind dwell on the simple truths that are before your eyes virtually all the time. I have already spoken of how I keep your heart going, breathe for you, transform your food into blood, bone, muscle, and brain. These are only a few of the things I do for you without help from you. Consider how I arranged for your body to absorb the healing and warming rays of the sun. The amazing communication system between your brain and all parts of your body is all my work. And so is the natural and perfect system of eliminating poisonous waste from your body, perfect until you clog it up by man-made interferences.

Consider the workings of the law of gravity which affect you continuously. Observe the passing of time; the moment that is here now is passing while you're considering it; you cannot recall it. Think of the changing seasons, spring, summer, fall, winter. The transition from light to darkness and to light again. The growth of plants for your food; man sows the seed, but the increase is my work. Meditate upon your own growth, from the time of conception to maturity, and your gradual descent and final passing from this earth.

* * *

Am I telling you these things to deflate you? To

humiliate you? To belittle the part you play in our Partnership? You know I am not. I seek only to have you learn the truth. The truth will make you free. It will also make you humble.

I seek only to have you learn of your true greatness. You and I are Partners. Together we can do great things. I need you. I cannot do my work on earth except through you. You cannot achieve your destiny except through Me. You and I have a great task before us.

We must overcome an enormous misconception that has overtaken mankind. In a recent survey 96% of Americans said they believe in Me. But when asked if they believed I had any interest in them personally, most of these people said "No." They believed that they stood alone, that God had left the world He had created and was waiting millions of miles off, to judge them some day.

* * *

The fallacy that man is an individual, going through life without the comforting presence of his Creative Partner, is largely responsible for the fact that one in every ten Americans suffers from mental disorder at one time or another. It is the ego part of you that worries and envies and becomes unhappy, never the Creative Spirit part of you. When you let your Partner guide you, you learn how to take adversity and suffering. These trials do not defeat but ennoble you. When faced with difficulties which defy all your efforts to solve, you learn to consent to what you must bear. You thus leave frustration behind and come out on top of your problems.

* * *

It is a tragic fact that your present system of education fails to get across to your youth the simple, basic truth that each has within him an infinite capacity for greatness, love and inner peace, and that this treasure can be claimed if self is made the servant of the Creative Spirit.

Having been cheated yourselves, you unwittingly cheat your children. You teach them that self-reliance means reliance on the ego, instead of what it truly means: reliance on my Spirit within. Your methods encourage children to exalt the personal self; the truth would give them a natural humility. Failing to understand where the true Source of power exists, your youth fall into your own error of worshipping the creature instead of the Creator.

This fatal separation from the Source that created and sustains you, that provided for your achievements and happiness, is at the heart of all problems.

* * *

The Partnership of man and Maker is no new concept. It was sponsored by the most practical man the world has ever known. Judged by what He said and by the way He lived, Christ came not to talk religion but to establish the living, working Partnership of man and Maker: "Knowest thou not that I am in the Father, and the Father in me? The things I do, I do not of my own. Of myself I am nothing. It is the Father within me that doeth the works."

At the time Christ said this the church was loaded down with formalisms. The orthodox religionists believed that God was in some distant heaven, sternly waiting to judge you. Christ challenged this. Repeatedly he admonished his people not to look here or there for God. "The Kingdom of God is within you." He made a case for the Partnership Life of man and Maker in such simple, understandable ways that great numbers of people accepted it. God's presence in man as a living, working Partner became the foundation stone of Christianity. "God created *in* man His image" became believable where the misinterpreted "God created man in His image" had caused confusion and misunderstanding. Formalism gave way to the Partnership Life, love of God and man.

* * *

Christ's followers discovered that He did all His work without strain or pressure. How? Simply because He knew the work was being done not *by* Him but *through* Him.

If you delude yourself that you are going it alone, you are bound to crack. You are putting yourself one step ahead of God. You can't hold that place or pace. This is plain common sense, not religion.

I am a Creative Spirit. My whole purpose in creating you and all human beings was to place my Spirit in you, so that we may live as One. I sent Christ to make clear to you that I am with you always. How often did He say, "The Kingdom of God is within you. . . . Don't look here or there." In the Book of John alone, Christ on 47 separate occasions emphasized that He never said anything, never did anything, never went anywhere except by My guidance. He gave His life to tell you of my eternal partnership with you.

Christ's teaching gives you the joy and power of Partnership with God. The early Christians understood and practiced Christ's partnership life. As instruments through whom I worked, they found their highest happiness. They loved and served one another.

Christ proved that the yielding of ego to God is no real loss. Is it a loss to surrender a part to gain the whole? Rather it is the one way to a full, joyous life. "I have come," Christ said, "that you might have my joy."

Every man who has ever accomplished anything worth while knows that the deed was achieved not *by* him but *through* him. "Let us take our bloated nothingness out of the path of the divine circuits. . . Men of an extraordinary success, in their honest moments, have always sung 'Not unto us, not unto us.' " Emerson wrote that. And Lincoln said this: "We are all agents and instruments of Divine Providence. . . Without the Divine assistance, I cannot succeed; with it, I cannot fail." The founding fathers, especially Washington, Franklin and Jefferson, had this same faith.

Most men today don't know their potential greatness; they leave this inner reservoir of power untapped. Passing through life so busy getting *things,* they have no time to get understanding and inner peace. If they would unshackle their minds, the true greatness lying dormant within them would free them from slavery to ego and make them as born anew—joyful and eager to serve their Partner and their fellow-man.

You are greater than you know. Infinitely greater. You are a living, working Partner of the Creative Power that sustains the universe. You were created in order that you might work a certain mission which no other human being can achieve. You may not be considered a "successful" person by the standard which asks only: "How much money have you?" "How important is your position?" "How well known are you?" But in the Partnership Life, a different success standard obtains. It asks: "How good a servant are you for your Partner, the Creator?" It makes no difference how humble your work or station. All that counts is that you let God work through you. You are then happy and successful. Your Maker gave you two hands, one to hold to Him, the other to your fellow-man. If your hands are full of—or struggling for—possessions, you can hold neither to God nor to humanity.

If you hold fast to Him who gave you life, who is your ever-present Partner, His loving Spirit will flow through you and out to your neighbor. That is the way to joy, love, achievement and inner peace.

Surely, if you love your children, you will teach them the simple truth of their own Partnership with

God. Therein lies their only real chance for a happy, fruitful life.

(*These were thoughts that seemed to come from my Partner. You alone can decide whether any of the thoughts which my Partner inspired in me have useful application in your life.*)

THE WAY

Breathe Out Ego, Breathe In God

A GOOD FRIEND said to me: "I like the Partnership concept. I wish I could believe in it whole-heartedly. But I am stopped by what seems to me a serious flaw: If the Creator is my ever-present, active Partner, why did He not provide a simple way for me to be conscious of His presence? Like many others, I have moments when I feel God near me. But in this workaday world, with all sorts of pressures upon us constantly, one has to be reminded right along of God's presence within him."

My friend went on: "I don't think it's a good answer to tell me that His presence should be accepted on faith; or that God can be seen in a tree, in the beauty of a flower or sunset, or even in the eyes of a child. These are all true, but they leave God outside of me." As my friend spoke, the words of Emerson came to me: "That which shows God in me fortifies me. That which shows God out of me makes me a wart and a wen. There is no longer a necessary reason for my being."

I had no answer for my friend. He pursued his point: "In the Partnership concept, you advance the proposition, and you make it sound as if it were beyond question, that God is within me, that He and I are partners. You say you build your case on practical grounds. Is it not fair to ask why God did not provide a simple and practical way by which I could keep reminded of

His presence? I mean a way as simple and natural as breathing."

My friend's question stuck in my mind. It became my own question. Pressing my Partner for the answer, I received at first only the gentle rebuke of Christ: "The Kingdom of God is within you. . . You have eyes and see not, ears and hear not, a mind and perceive not." But I was not satisfied. Christ's faith was such that He saw God in everything and felt His presence within. He needed no reminding. But the rest of us need evidence of a more tangible nature. Why is a way not provided to remember God? And if it is provided, why do we have such a time discovering it?

Later the way was shown to me. It came at a time when I was not trying to find the answer. My efforts were being directed to getting myself out of my Partner's way; I felt sure that when I had achieved a certain growth, my Partner would flow the answer through me, and it would be, as my friend said, "as simple as breathing." Quite unconsciously I heaved a sigh. As I did, from somewhere came the thought: "Out, ego." With the incoming breath, the thought came clear: "In, God."

There was the way!

It was not only as simple as breathing; breathing *was* the way! Proof of God's presence in man could be found in the very air we breathe. Breathing is divided into two parts: out and in. Out, when we may breathe out ego; in, when we may breathe in God.

My Partner now began to instruct me in some research work into the mystery which we call "air." He showed me that this invisible substance is an amazing combination of the physical and the spiritual.

(*Again, with the few noted exceptions, all that follows in this chapter are thoughts that seemed to come from my Partner:*)

With every breath of air you breathe in life-giving oxygen for your body and you also breathe in the very Spirit of God. The words "breath" and "spirit" come from the same stem. The Latin word "*spirare*," meaning to breathe, is the root of the English word "spirit," by which you designate the all-pervading Power which creates and sustains the universe. Air, invisible as God Himself, is the breath of life, I, your Creator breathed into you at the beginning. It is the spiritual life blood flowing every second from the Creator to you. The physical umbilical cord is severed at birth, but air is a "cord" that ties you to Me, your Maker, your whole life long.

Air is a complete integration of the material and the spiritual, an ever-present reminder of the Partnership of your physical self with the Creative Spirit.

Air is the one physical thing that unceasingly, uninterruptedly flows between you and your Maker. When air stops flowing between your body and Him, death follows. "Thou takest away their breath, they die, and return to their dust."

The Spirit of Life rides in the air you breathe. Ever flowing into you and out of you, air is proof in itself of your Creative Partner's plan to be with you in every thought and deed.

Having made air the connecting link between Him and you, the Creator wanted nothing to interfere with this lifeline. He did not give you any choice in the matter. You cannot escape breathing. You may for a while do without the Creator's other gifts, food, water, sun and sleep, but you cannot do without air. Even when you hold your breath, it is the oxygen already in your blood that keeps you going until the next breath.

Everything in creation—"books in running brooks, sermons in stones and good in everything"—testifies to God's presence everywhere, but in air God provided the answer to all doubts as to His constant presence within you.

Asleep or deep in thought, during an important business deal or in a time of crisis, you are constantly breathing in air. You may not have given much thought to the air you breathe. Daniel Webster observed that most people "hardly take heed of that atmosphere which supports their lives from day to day and from hour to hour." But a little meditation reveals that air is the Creator's assurance of His constant Presence and Partnership with man, and that breathing is what God counts on to ensure man's constant consciousness of his complete dependence on his Maker.

You know something of air's physical properties. Air is no imaginary substance. It is real. It has weight. It has volume. It supports great planes weighing many tons. Air plays a part in the construction of every product, natural and man-made.

These are aspects of the material side of air, but greater by far are its spiritual qualities. In the air you breathe is the soul of the universe. With each breath you take, you breathe in the intelligence which directs the course of the planets through the vast reaches of space. Every breath of air carries with it not only life itself but the very love and power of God.

Before attempting to breathe in God, you must first empty yourself of ego. With ego out, you can't help but breathe in God. First breathe out ego, then breathe in God. Breathe out care, breathe in peace of mind. Breathe out weakness, breathe in strength.

I created air in order that my Spirit may enter into you in an uninterrupted flow. You ask for proof of my Presence within you. *Air offers that proof.* You ask for a way to be reminded of my Partnership with you. *Breathing is that way.* I could have made breathing as independent of your will as the beating of your heart. I do entirely take over the work of breathing during your sleep. But it is my hope and plan that in your conscious moments it will become a joint act of our Partnership. The benefits you will derive from the simple practice of breathing out ego, breathing in God will seem a miracle to you. Your body will be made younger, your mind clearer, and your spirit ennobled. You will be transformed.

It was no accident that I made breathing a joint action, you and I working together as partners. I in-

tended that you should arrive at the truth about Me
first through your intellect, not that you should de-
mand to see Me with your eyes. You cannot see the
air you breathe, yet you know it is there. Is the Creator
of air less real than the air He created? You know
that air is within you. Can you doubt that the Creator
of air is within you? Air surrounds you everywhere.
It is impossible for you to be where air is not. How
can you be where the Creator is not? It is through
air that you both hear and speak. Do you think that
you are able to converse with people but unable to converse with the Creator of both air and people?

My purpose in creating breathing was to keep man
ever mindful of my partnership with him. Here is
the proof you demanded. Believe it with all your heart.
Breathe out doubt as you breathe out ego. And breathe
out all other by-products of ego: cares, worries, aches,
vanities. Then, having made room for Me, breathe in
the Creative Spirit whose one intention is to help you
live a full, rich life, in vigorous health, at peace with
yourself and your fellow-man.

You recall how you had attempted to follow the advice of psychologists to live one day at a time. "Live
in daytight compartments" they urged. This was
sound advice. It meant to live each day at a time, not
borrowing trouble from the days yet to come. But
once learning to breathe out ego, breathe in God, you
strive to live in *airtight* compartments, one breath at
a time. This helps one to live in the Eternal Now, concentrating on the needs of the moment, leaving no

room for regrets for the past or fears for the future. In the hands of God all problems find their proper solution.

Obviously the change in you does not come about as the result of one breath; it comes as the result of sincere practice. If it is your soul's sincere desire to let your Partner "take over your life," the practice of breathing out ego, breathing in God cannot fail. Only one thing is necessary, and that is to get yourself out of your Partner's way. All things then fall into their proper place. If this seems too simple, too good to be true, remember that it is not *you* working this miracle. It is your Partner, your Maker, and with Him all things are possible. "Seek ye first the Kingdom of God and all things shall be added unto you."

There will be times without number when you will forget my Presence within you and try to "take over" yourself. There will be even more occasions when you will forget to practice breathing out ego, breathing in God. Your Partner knows this. Though you fail again and again, God will reach down, take you by the hand and help you start again. But you cannot hold to both ego and God. Both cannot be your Masters.

The standard of success which you have hitherto revered is an abomination in my sight. But if the desire for money, position, fame, has you in its grip and you desire sincerely to be freed, your Partner will help you win the fight. Did He refuse help to the man who openly confessed: "I believe: help Thou mine unbelief"? You need not be eloquent toward Me. Only sincere. So begin now, no matter how feebly or uncertainly, the practice of breathing out ego, breathing in God. Soon you will feel a glow of warmth as you breathe, as if the Everlasting Arms were enfolding you.

You will determine then and there that henceforth in every crisis, great or small, your first move will be to breathe out ego, breathe in God. Thus you implement your own limited strength and vision with that of the eternal Creative Power with whom all things are possible. If a difficulty facing you seems unbearable, with your outgoing breath you remember, "This, too, shall pass." And then you breathe in the great peace that only your Partner, the great Healer, can give.

* * *

You grow more conscious of the simple truth that to breathe is to live. Without breath there is no life. It is true from the beginning. An infant emerges from the womb, sucks in the life-giving air, lets out a wail, and begins life on earth. The aged person gives a faint gasp, ceases to breathe, and life is over. Life is a series of breaths.

An intelligent use of your breathing power will lengthen your days on earth and give you increased vitality and powers of resistance. Failure properly to use your breathing power will shorten your days, decrease your vitality and lower your immunity to disease.

Have you ever pondered on the part you call upon Me to play in supplying you the breath of life 16 times each minute, 960 times each hour, 23,040 times each day. In one day approximately 35,000 pints of blood traverse the capillaries of the lungs, each blood corpuscle passing in single file, and being exposed to the oxygen of the air on both surfaces. How can this fail to compel awe and wonder at the Creator's infinite care and the perfection of His plan? You see how important it is for fresh air to reach the lungs in sufficient quantities to purify the foul stream of venous blood. Otherwise the body is robbed of nourishment, and waste products which should be destroyed and eliminated are returned to circulation, poisoning the system and bringing about illness and premature death. Proper breathing provides the further benefit of good exercise for the internal organs and muscles, promoting good circulation and a clear, bright complexion.

Some of the benefits of breathing are the result of the physical properties of air; others cannot be so explained. Proper breathing accomplishes more than the mere oxygenation of the blood. Air contains more than oxygen and other invisible, odorless and tasteless gases. There is a certain very real spiritual quality in air, for which your eastern brothers have a very convenient word, "prana." Prana is the vital force which creates and sustains life. It is of the Creative Spirit. In its absence you would die, even if your system were filled with the other components of air. The presence of prana makes air the complete integration of the physical and spiritual.

Now you know why the practice of breathing out ego, breathing in God gives you a reservoir of strength for emergencies. The prana you take in with every breath is stored up just as electricity is stored in a storage battery. When you are faced with a crisis which might otherwise break your spirit and leave you embittered, your stored-up prana flows out to your support, bringing you faith and strength. Every part of you feels its power and love and peace. The brain receives increased energy and tranquility from this reservoir of God's Spirit. Unconsciously you radiate a vitality and strength that is communicated to all who come in contact with you. By means of prana Christ healed the sick. In His loving glance there was magnetic healing power. Some selfless souls today have this power to a limited degree. It is possible actually to feel the love and power of personal magnetism emanating from such.

Some of your technically trained friends may smile at these things. In their laboratories they are unable to find any trace of prana; it does not register on their instruments. But is there any known way scientifically to determine the presence or effects of love? Prana is real, as love is real, as God is real.

As the oxygen in the air is appropriated by the blood and used by the circulatory system, so prana in the air is appropriated and used by the nervous system. As oxygenated blood is carried to all parts of the system, building and replenishing, so prana is carried to all parts of the nervous system, bringing strength, vitality and tranquility. Prana is a spiritual force which is above and beyond the present understanding of man. Prana lies behind the wonderful beauty and simplicity and power that reside in a breath of air. And prana is free and available to all.

Should you not resolve henceforth that with every breath, you will breathe out ego, breathe in God? In this practice you will discover and come into harmony with the great natural rhythm which pervades the universe. It is the same rhythm that is in the swing of the planets around the sun; in the rise and fall of the sea; in the beating of the heart; in the ebb and flow of the tide. When you breathe out ego, breathe in God, you fall in with this cosmic rhythm. You become the beneficiary of its inspiration, its power, its love and its peace.

(My Partner now instructed me further in simple natural ways to practice breathing. I found that when I began my exercise by breathing out, I made room for the incoming breath to fill my lungs, and every part of my body seemed to respond to this incoming draft of air. When I thoroughly emptied my lungs, a strenuous effort was not needed to fill them again. My Partner did that for me. I co-operated with Him in this phase of breathing, but my part was small by comparison with His. I seemed just to flow along with Him, in a natural and effortless manner.

So I begin by heaving a sigh, at the same time trying to make my shoulder blades meet at the back. This helps to force out the stale, toxic air. I think of it also as forcing out the ego. At the same time there is a pulling in and narrowing of the abdomen and waist line. When the incoming breath has filled me with God's love and power, this wonderful Partnership act has completed one cycle, only to start another in which I again breathe out ego, breathe in God. I initiate the outgoing breath, He the incoming breath. It is as simple as that.

This is not an "expert's" method, but it has worked for me. After one week, I was sold on its value, spiritually, physically, mentally. Now after several years' practice, I must again seriously tell you that I look upon it as the greatest discovery of my life, save only the discovery of my Partnership with God.

It helps in my practice to think of my breathing apparatus in terms of a rubber ball with holes in it, the holes being the nostrils. Squeeze the ball and air is forced through the holes. Release your grip on the ball, and it slowly fills with air. Observe that the air sifts into the ball without any aid from you. "Nature abhors a vacuum" and air rushes in to fill the partial vacuum caused by squeezing the ball. In my outward breath, I feel as if the breathing apparatus were being squeezed; the air is forced through the nostrils, which serve as exhaust vents to rid the body of gaseous, toxic impurities.

The change of air within my body does physical wonders for me. The change from ego to God works both spiritual and material wonders. Having now fol-

lowed the practice of breathing out ego, breathing in God for a period of several years, I can testify to its indescribable benefits. It has been a source of the greatest aid and comfort under every condition of life confronting me. It has blessed and healed me. It has guided me over many rough places. I regard it as proof of God's Partnership plan of man and Maker. This assurance grows with each passing day. My Partner's words to me dwell often on this great discovery:)

Practice the presence of God in this way anywhere and everywhere, any time and all the time. Soon it will become a habit, a largely unconscious habit, yet you will always be aware of the great lift it gives you. Certain times will be more opportune for practice than others. On such occasions you may want to close your eyes and breathe out deeply. So great will be your Partner's rush to fill you with His love that you will feel Him enter through what seem to be closed lips. The air will seem bent on reaching the outermost portions of your body, bringing with it new life and a wonderful peace. When these waves of God flow into you, they provide an experience of such inspiration, power and beauty as to be almost unbelievable.

Sometimes you will want to practice deep breathing when walking in the open fields, or in a city park, or by a stream, or on a mountain trail. The radiant glow thus brought to your face is but a reflection of the radiance in your heart. As you breathe out ego, breathe in God, you will find yourself echoing the psalmist's words: "I will lift up mine eyes unto the hills whence cometh my strength."

Sometimes you will be inspired to practice as you walk the streets of a large city, oblivious to all the materialism about you. By concentrating on breathing out ego, breathing in God, you rise above your problems. Such a feeling of love for others comes upon you that you wish it were possible to embrace all mankind and pass on to them understanding of the great joy that would be theirs from this simple practice of the presence of God.

On such occasions you will have so grown as a channel for your Partner that your thought will be, "Breathe out love for others, breathe in God's love for me." This will represent a tremendous advance in your progress toward one-ness with God. As you grow more in love for His other children, you grow toward the achievement of the purpose for which you were created.

* * *

What everyday benefits are to be expected from the practice of breathing out ego, breathing in God? Your own experiences will supply the answers.

In Illness

IN ILLNESS, the effects of breathing out ego, breathing in God are dramatic and often miraculous. If you are confined to your bed and in pain, this sincere practice will bring you great physical, mental and spiritual benefits.

(*A cancerous skin growth on my chest was removed, leaving an open area of more than six inches in length and several inches wide. The surgeon despaired of its healing, after several attempts to sew it up had failed. It healed naturally. Dr. Alexis Carrel, Nobel Prize winner in surgery, told how he could never forget seeing a cancerous sore miraculously shrivel to a scar before his eyes. My healing did not occur that fast, but I am persuaded that the same Power, responding to the same kind of faith, was the Healer.*)

Particularly in illness it is good to know that with every outgoing breath you can drive away thoughts and pain of self, and with every incoming breath, you can bring closer to you the one Power that gives peace of mind and relief from suffering. The Master promised that your faith will make you whole. But faith, St. James said, must be accompanied by works. Do not sit back and ask God to do it all. Particularly do not disregard the simple natural laws for health. You place an almost intolerable burden on faith if you violate physical laws while you appeal for spiritual help.

God created your body and provided the things necessary to sustain it in good health. So while you breathe out ego and breathe in God, do not feed your body devitalized and unbalanced foods. Vigorous health depends largely on the delicate balance of wholeness I have placed in foods. This balance is upset if the soil or food has been robbed of life-giving elements.

Follow your Partner's way and He will help you in your illness. He will give you strength and peace. You will feel the warmth of His love, the power of His presence. There is no limitation on God's power to heal unless you yourself put it there. You hinder Him if you do not place yourself unconditionally in His hands. You hinder Him when you ask for specific conditions. Unwittingly you hold to ego while appealing to Him.

Breathe out ego completely. Remove it utterly from your thoughts. Make of yourself a servant for the Will of God. Mean it with all your heart when you say: "Thy Will, not mine." Thus you clear the way for your Partner. Have you not good reason to trust Him completely? Of all your possessions is He not the Giver? He wants you to be healthy and happy. He needs you in His work. Your faith in Him will make you whole. Brother Lawrence wrote: "If we were well accustomed to the exercise of the presence of God, all bodily diseases would be much alleviated thereby."

As you breathe in God's Spirit, peace will fill your soul. It will flood your mind, and its healing power will be felt in every part of your body. This is the peace that passes all understanding. Pain that was before unendurable now becomes endurable, and in time, in your Partner's own time, the pain will leave you.

Let no one persuade you to belittle the power that lies in a breath of air. "Is it not your breath," wrote Gibran in *The Prophet,* "that has erected and hardened the structure of your bones?... Could you but see the tides of that breath, you would cease to see all else."

In sickness and in health, the tides of your breath are a constant reminder of how great is your dependence on your Maker, of how much all human beings draw from the same source, of how you are all brothers. You are children of the one Father who has tied you to Him with invisible breaths of air, so that you come to Him each moment to renew your life. Earlier I spoke to you of prana, that invisible ingredient in every breath of air. Be not disturbed by the mystical sound of prana. Like The Light, it is but another expression of the Creative Spirit. The breath of life is also the breath of health. So breathe it in, and become whole. But first breathe out self. Then breathe in selfless power. Breathe out sickness, breathe in health. Soon you'll be breathing out love for others, breathing in God's love for you.

When You Can't Sleep

THE HOUR IS somewhere between two and four in the morning. You have been awake for some time. Your mind is running on and on. The burdens of the world are upon you. Things have not been going well; you have not been feeling up to par physically; bills are piling up; there are worries both at home and in the office. Your wife may not have been very understanding of late, possibly because you have not been very companionable. Your daughter is at an age that is full of problems. Your boy would like to go to medical school, which means a long pull at several thousand per year. Maybe the hydrogen bomb will end everything, anyhow.

You toss from side to side. All you are thinking about is how to forget all you are thinking about. If only you could get some good sound sleep, things would seem different in the morning. But you can't sleep. You'll get up in the morning dreading the things that must be done. How long can you take this? You don't want to fall back on sleeping pills every night. There must be some answer.

There is. It is the same as the answer to all problems: get yourself out of the way and let your Partner take over. For you have a Partner, whether you know it or not—the Creator who brought you into existence and who sustains you every moment. He integrated His Spirit with your being in an eternal, active Partnership. If you choose to disbelieve this, you make it difficult for your Partner to help you. But has He not been known to disregard such barriers and come to the aid of His children anyhow, expecting perhaps they may discover Him in a blessing where they could not find Him in suffering?

Try to realize that there is a Power within you far greater than your own, the Power that is keeping your heart beating. Then begin quietly to breathe out ego, the one force that blocks your Partner's efforts to help you. Breathe out ego with such determination that you can feel it traveling away from you in no uncertain manner. Then slowly breathe in God. Breathe Him in with all the love and gratitude of which you are capable. Open your heart to the eternal Creative Power. Welcome His Spirit so wholeheartedly that He enters into every part of your being.

Breathe out ego again, easily but as resolutely as before. Visualize the unwanted character of egotism as being hustled away from your presence and taken far away. Then breathe in God again, gently. The great loving Spirit fills you and takes hold of you. His soothing, healing influence extends throughout your body. With each succeeding breath, you are conscious less of self, more of your Divine Partner.

Now, as you keep practicing the breathing out of ego, the breathing in of God, you experience a growing sense of relaxation. You stop worrying about not sleeping. You realize that it is not necessary to lose consciousness in order to be refreshed. You find that it is quite possible to rest more thoroughly while awake and relaxed than while asleep, particularly if the sleep is fitful or induced by sleeping pills. In due time the practice of breathing out ego, breathing in God, will bring about a night of *real* sleep.

When you awaken from such a sleep, your mind as well as your body is rested. You feel alive, joyous, grateful, inspired. The day ahead is something to look forward to! You lie there quietly and give silent thanks. While you breathe out ego, breathe in God, you ask yourself why you cannot always be like this. Why all the worry, the confusion, the constant feeling of pressure? You see that it all comes from the self-delusion of being self-made and self-sustained. In truth, no man stands alone. If his next few breaths of air were withheld, he would quickly die.

You realize that the stupid rat race you are living is getting you nowhere. You are wearing yourself out, going at things as if you were a factory. You resolve that from now on you will be an instrument for your Partner. You will be a channel; your Partner will flow through you, guiding and blessing you as you do His work. As water flowing through a channel enriches the soil which it traverses, so will you be enriched as your Partner flows through you. You will be able to do far more and better work when He is guiding you than when you delude yourself that you can work alone. And so the day begins on a high note of quiet confidence. "In quietness and confidence shall be my strength." Rugged individualism has given way to the Partnership truth. Tasting the joy of it, you begin now to practice your great discovery often during the day.

* * *

Breathing out ego, breathing in God to beget peaceful sleep is no man-made escape mechanism like counting sheep. Breathing out ego, breathing in God is a positive, dynamic and natural solution to all your problems. *For all your problems lie in your ego.* The projection of ego into God's affairs—butting into God's business—causes *all* your trouble. Get the ego out of God's way, and He will dispose of your trouble, whatever it may be.

When you combine the words "ego" and "God," you get a coined word—EGOD—that is strangely symbolic of the real relationship of ego and God. Every man has been given freedom to decide which is to be "boss" of his Partnership. If you insist on first place for yourself, you silence the last letter of EGOD so that your Partnership is pronounced EGO. If you choose willingly to surrender leadership to your Partner, you silence the first letter of EGOD, pronouncing your Partnership GOD. Your sincere willingness to take last place qualifies you for full Partnership.

It is as if both Partners, EGO and GOD, were on opposite ends of a kind of slide rule. Work the slide rule and you find that the more of EGO, the less of GOD; the less of EGO, the more of GOD. This is a law, no man can change it. Many men in their mid-forties and early fifties are cracking today because, contrary to the law of their being, they are trying to stand alone. Abraham Lincoln said: "I was early brought to a living reflection that nothing in my power whatever, in others to rely upon, would succeed without the direct assistance of the Almighty—but all must fail."

So breathe out ego, breathe in God. Out self, in Divine Spirit. Out worry, in peace. You will soon feel the soothing, blessed effects of God's presence. Your mind becomes clean and clear and understanding. Love fills your heart. Tiredness and sleeplessness leave you. You feel as if you have rested a long time. A glow comes upon you. A peace of mind. Everything is going to be all right now. "There is a spirit in man; and the breath of the Almighty giveth him understanding."

Let this discovery take precedence over all other desires and ambitions. Breathe out ego, breathe in God. Do it for one day, and when you lie down for your nightly rest the Everlasting Arms will gather you in and give you a night of peace. Do it for one week and you will come upon a sureness that the Partnership Life works. Do it for one month and others will see in you the great change you feel in yourself.

In Frustration

It HAS BEEN WISELY observed that the true measure of a man is how much it takes to "get his goat." A better measure may be how he reacts to a frustration offering no hope of solution.

Without a faith to live by, any man can be broken down by continued frustration. Most people can bear temporary setbacks. There must be losers in the various encounters in the game of life, and people expect to have their share of losses. But when something on which you have worked long and hard, something very dear to your heart, meets with a sudden and unexpected frustration which precludes any attempt at solution, the trial can be agonizing indeed. To the man who "stands alone" the situation may appear hopeless. It is not so with him who knows that he has as his Partner an allwise and loving Creator. The frustration is soon placed in proper perspective.

To place "first things first" in your own mind, nothing is more helpful than the practice of breathing out ego, breathing in God. When news of the frustration comes, it may be at a time when you are not alone and cannot get alone. That is when past practice of breathing out ego, breathing in God stands you in good stead. Almost instinctively you move to get yourself out of the picture, so that it may become a true picture. You breathe out ego; then slowly you breathe in God. If possible you remain silent, letting others talk if they choose, while you concentrate on trying to let Me, your Partner, take over.

Thus it will not be long before the particular thing which loomed so large to you finds its proper place in the scheme of things. And its place is never where ego would put it, so close to your vision that all else would be blotted out.

You realize that this problem, important as it seemed, is *not* the most immediate thing in your affairs. Nothing is more immediate than the breath you are about to take. Nothing is more important, nothing more pressing.

For when you have breathed yourself out, the incoming breath will not rest, will not wait. It is all-compelling. It demands to get into you *now,* and it will not be denied. To refuse it would be to invite death. You cannot plead the press of affairs or the fact that you have just received the shock of your life; it would be of no avail. The incoming breath takes precedence over everything in your life, for it *is* your life. It is the life-giving breath of your Partner. In it is all the power and magic of God's Creative Spirit. Treat it casually if you will, even with the disrespect born of ignorance. But beware of treating it with derision and scorn, for this is blasphemy. All manner of sins will be forgiven you, said the Master, except one: blasphemy of the Holy Spirit within you. This is the unforgivable sin. The basis of true Christianity is faith in the presence of God within man, and to hold this up to ridicule is to mock the deepest truth.

So when you take the incoming breath that will not be denied, do it with full consciousness that God is coming in with it. Do not place yourself among the "unthinking or the careless" of whom Daniel Webster spoke, who give no heed to the breath of air that supports them from hour to hour and minute to minute.

You may have temporary lapses in your effort to breathe out ego and breathe in God. But in the long run the practice never fails. So keep trying. Keep practicing. Even though you forget time and again, earnestly return and try again.

Breathing goes on within you anyhow. Take a conscious part in it during your waking hours. Make it the Partnership affair it was created to be. Gather unto yourself the great benefits that come from breathing out ego, breathing in God. Mean it with all your heart. Your Partner will respond if you aspire with a sincere heart. He will not fail you. *But neither will He be fooled.* You cannot hold on to ego while trying to get Him to help you. What counts with your Partner is the spirit with which you attempt this great transformation. You must be sincere. He does not mind your failures, but deceit He will not take. He knows your heart. It is futile to be other than wholly honest.

In dealing with frustrations it may help to remember that the world was here several billions of years before you made your appearance upon it. It will continue long after your body will have returned to the earth from which it came. As eternity is measured, your stay on earth is but a fleeting second. And even if the ambition in which you have been frustrated was a most worthy one, perhaps one in which you hoped to serve your fellow-man, there is no cause to lose faith in your Partner. He has other and better plans for you. His Spirit is still with you and will guide you in the right path at the right time. You are His temple. "Knowest thou not that thy body is a temple for the Holy Spirit?" Your desire is to be a temple in which He can dwell, a channel through which He can pour His loving work.

As you come to understand your right place in the Partnership plan, you realize that it is a vital one. Your Partner needs your hands to do His work. But you realize that yours is not the number one spot. That is your Partner's place. When you are tempted to take over, start without delay to breathe out ego, breathe in God. Thus you open up the way for your Partner to do His work. Thus you are enabled to help others, and thus, through giving joy to others, you find your own joy.

In Anger

ANGER IS THE handmaiden of frustration. In the heat
of anger, bitter words are said; injuries are done;
crimes are committed. In the prevention of anger's
terrible damage, the habit of breathing out ego, breathing in God, is an immensely valuable help. Angry
deeds and words are withheld when you practice the
presence of God for any length of time.

Anger is simply ego taking over. It is a very stub-
born difficulty. People with a low boiling point need
the help of a Power greater than their own. A quick
temper can be overcome only when a sincere effort is
made to submerge one's ego.

But how about righteous anger? Is that not justi-
fiable? Anger is righteous only if it is entirely selfless.
Righteous anger is never hot or uncontrollable. Righteous anger is aroused only by man's inhumanity to
man. It is productive of no sudden violence or desire
to harm, but only a sincere effort to mend a wrong.
It is easy to be deceived on this point. Righteous anger
is very rare.

It is not enough to control anger if you still burn
within. This form of suppression can prove even
worse than blowing off steam. You may fool yourself but you do not fool your Partner. He knows what
is in your mind and heart. Christ said that the man
who looks upon a woman with lust is really commit-

ting adultery. The man who looks upon another with hatred in his heart is in a sense committing the crime he is considering. Moreover, he is doing himself greater harm than the one he hates.

True self-control is control of the lower self by the Higher Self, control of ego by God. So keep breathing out ego, and with it breathe out all the things that cling to ego: ambition, vanity, lust for power, anger, repression. Then breathe in the great loving Power, the Power that created and sustains the universe, the Power that created and sustains you. Feel this Power filling your whole being with strength and love. Reflect on the easy spontaneous way in which this Power works in the rising and setting of the sun, in the emergence of the moon and stars at night, in the planting and growth of a seed, in miracles beyond your imagination.

Reflect on how easily things work out when you make yourself a channel through which the great Power works. You are not called upon to humiliate yourself. Humility is not humiliation. Your Partner respects and needs you. It is only a question of your proper place in the Partnership. Do you really think that God should be your vice-president? Don't you have to smile at the thought of it?

Your whole burden is to be a good Partner to God. Taking guidance from Him is a yoke you take on cheerfully and gratefully, for you have the most complete faith in His leadership. You know everything will work out for your good.

You begin to understand why Christ's yoke was easy and His burden light. He did not carry the burden. He let the Father do that. His faith and trust were such that He knew He had only to get self out of the way and the Father would work through Him.

As Christ promised, when you give up ego you give up the burdens of self. When your ego lets go, God takes over. It is ego that builds up frustrations, repressions and anger. It is ego that makes a pressure factory of your mind, a factory that rapidly wears you out. Breathe out the pressure factory. Breathe in the gently flowing Grace of God. Out factory. In grace.

In Your Relations With
Family and Friends

HAVE BEAUTY AND enthusiasm gone out of your life?
Is life at home a humdrum affair? A place where you
eat, watch TV and sleep? Where your children take
you as a matter of course and sometimes get on your
nerves? Or is your home a place where love abides?
Where thoughtfulness and consideration and gratitude
are in the very atmosphere? The home where love
abides is a home where God is breathed in with the air.
That is what makes a loving atmosphere, the presence
of God.

Would there be a divorce in every three marriages
if people breathed out ego, breathed in God? Divorces
are the direct result of ego at work. Incompatibility
usually is two egos working hard at being egos.

Unfortunately the whole trend of modern life is to
exalt ego and keep it in first place. The act of breathing out ego, breathing in God is more than a form of
self-renunciation. It is losing one's lower life in order
to find a higher life. Those about you will respond to
this higher life as if it were magic, which indeed it is.
Beaming out love to others, it hits the mark like radar
and comes back enriched a thousand fold. This is one
of life's most amazing experiences.

Your fellow-man is also breathing in prana, that
divine ingredient which the Creator put in the air. All

human beings breathe air from the one common source. All breathe out to that one supply. The same air that bathes and caresses you bathes and caresses your fellow-man. Air that a moment ago was in you is now in your neighbor. Can you see in this God's plan to draw you closer both to your Maker and to your fellow-man?

People living long distances from you may be closer than you think. High, strong winds may carry to you air that a remote stranger was breathing only a short while ago; now it becomes a part of you. No man is an island unto himself. Air makes you all part of the mainland. God decreed that you cannot hold on to the breath you have just taken. In order to live, you must give it away. Thus He makes it clear that in order to live you must give.

The practice of breathing out ego, breathing in God, is a constant proof and reminder that God is Life and God is Love. God is Life because He breathed into you the breath of life and with each breath He renews that life. God is Love because in sustaining you each moment He shows His love.

When you breathe out ego, breathe in God, you show your love for your fellow-men. Seeing in you something new and radiant, they will want this radiance for themselves. You help each one, drawing no lines between God's children. You respect all persons, seeing in them the same Partner you have.

You realize the beauty of God's plan in making breathing a two-way affair. You come to God at in-

tervals for food and water, but there is no pause in
your coming for air. You are never separated from
your source of supply. He who made you is always
with you. He is your ever-present, loving Partner. If
you aspire to make the most of your life, if you would
show Him your gratitude, keep practicing breathing
out ego, breathing in God.

In Meeting With Success

Most people can take adversity because they must. But success carries with it elements that can easily get under your guard. You purr inwardly or puff outwardly over your own superiority. But the man who is conscious of his Partnership with God is protected in a great measure against the insidious dangers of success. He knows the true source of any ability he may have, and praise cannot get to him to do its damage.

The man who is unaware of his partnership with his Maker has only his own common sense and powers of analysis to protect him, talents which often do not prevail against the weapons that success has in its armory. Lacking the armor of God, the egocentric man is vulnerable to the honors heaped upon him by well-wishing friends.

The practice of breathing out ego, breathing in God, offers the greatest possible protection against these dangers. It makes of success the basis of a deep sense of gratitude.

In your heart you are devoutly thankful for the blessings that have come your way, and you see the hand of your Partner in all of them. You are thankful for God's gifts of air, sunshine, rain, food, friends, family, and work. You are thus in a much stronger position to endure "success" than the one who has taken the blessings of God for granted.

In Keeping Young and Well

Breathing out ego, breathing in God, will help you keep well and make you feel younger. You will be convinced of this fact in a very short time after beginning your practice.

Age is less a matter of years than a matter of condition. Some men in their sixties are younger than others in their forties. The half-well man of forty often looks and feels older than the well man of sixty. In a very real sense, he *is* the older of the two.

Because the practice of breathing out ego, breathing in God, leads directly to living the Partnership Life, you are guided to better and more wholesome living. Your Partner enables you more readily to resist the temptations of foods that tend to deplete your natural resistance to ailments. As you gradually acquire a natural immunity to the ravages of over-civilization, you wonder at the simplicity and majesty of your Partner's ways: how He strengthens your body; how He lifts you above cares and worries; how He gives you peace of mind.

You come to understand that His simple laws pertain to everything in you, your body, your mind, your spirit. You recognize that all three are integrated; what affects one, affects the others. Just observing His laws for one aspect of yourself is not enough. Life is a whole and your Partner works in wholeness. Man fragments his life, dividing it into compartments, but when he lets go and allows his Partner to take over God can and does make him whole.

Breathing out ego, breathing in God, is no cute trick or self-hypnosis stunt. It is no effort to convince yourself that "day by day in every way I am getting better and better." It is not an attempt to affirm the positive in order to overcome the negative. It is not a method of recovering health by denying the existence of the physical body. It is not trying to lift yourself by your bootstraps.

Breathing out ego, breathing in God, is a forthright, sincere effort to reinstate the truth. In breathing out ego you are seeking to rid yourself of the false, the spurious, the impostor. In breathing in God you are attempting to breathe in the essence of all creation, the source of all life, wisdom, and love. Thus you are acknowledging the simple truth that you are neither self-created nor self-sustained, that you depend on the creative power of God every moment to furnish the breath of life without which you would perish.

Breathing out ego, breathing in God, is conscious cooperation in your reception of prana, the invisible spiritual quality in air which has illimitable power. Prana, the divine aroma, is far more life-giving than any known element. It is "that of God in every man." Under the influence of prana your mind becomes clearer and your body is cleansed and strengthened. Prana enables you to manifest the presence of your Partner in a transformed mind and redeemed body.

With the quickening of your consciousness you

realize that the act of breathing was intended by your Creator to be a symbol of the highest significance, a symbol of His Partnership with you. More than anything else you do, breathing is an act performed by you and your Maker together. It is an act that must be repeated continuously. Your Maker, aware of your need to be reminded each moment of His presence within you, created breathing as that reminder. Could there be a better way to make clear His Partnership Plan. . . to make you aware that He is always with you, closer than hands and feet. . . to demonstrate your complete dependence upon Him. . . to keep you humble and grateful?

In a democracy, each elected representative must come to the people every few years to obtain a new lease on his job. Your Maker requires you to come to Him every few seconds for a new lease on life. All of man's troubles stem from disregarding, knowingly or unknowingly, the Creator's part in sustaining the life He has created. So breathe out ego, breathe in God. Breathe out the foolish and narrow viewpoints of self. Breathe in the large vision of your Maker and Partner. Breathe out the petty cares that bring on premature age and breakdown. Breathe in the unspeakable joy and power that make and keep you young. Breathe out the thoughts of material bread and breathe in the true bread of life, the Spirit of God.

No defect in heredity, no unfortunate environment, can prove impervious to the steady practice of breathing out ego, breathing in God. The bad, the weak and the defective are driven out; in their place the good, the strong and the perfect are introduced. You will experience the miracle of feeling your body grow younger. Your spiritual development will enable you to get along on less food, because the food you do eat will be more life-giving. Your stomach will diminish in size and in importance. At the same time your breathing capacity will gain in both size and importance. Your chest will expand while your waist line contracts.

You will grow more and more immune to common ailments like colds, headaches, faulty elimination and rheumatic pains. You will find yourself better able to withstand cold weather, thriving on it rather than running from it.

But the great physical benefits from the practice of breathing out ego, breathing in God, are small compared to the rewards your inner spirit receives. You become a new man in every sense of the word. Invisible air, the complete integration of the physical and spiritual, literally builds you anew. It is so simple as to seem unbelievable to those who make life complex. But the Creator always works in simple ways—so simple they seem mysterious—His wonders to perform.

In Money Matters

F EARS ABOUT money can be among the most haunting and relentless of all fears. You want security for yourself and your loved ones. You have certain needs, and you work hard to provide for them. The desire for security is natural. But there is a great fallacy in believing that man on his own can achieve security.

A wealthy man in an eastern city sought to make his young son completely secure. He had his large and beautiful estate fenced in and equipped with a playground, a swimming pool, a gymnasium and a school room. A tutor came each weekday to give the boy his education. To make sure that no harm could come to the lad, he was always surrounded by caretakers. But one day a ball the boy was bouncing took an odd hop and went through the iron spiked fence into the street, and before anyone could stop him the child opened a gate, dashed into the street after the ball, was struck by a car and killed. In a matter of seconds, the father's efforts of many years to insure security for his son had been brushed aside.

In another city a capable and prudent business man had prepared a long time for his retirement. Efficient to the point of coldness, he made meticulous plans. He bought a home in Florida where he would live six months. He bought another home in New England and a new car to ply between his two residences. But on the morning of the day he was scheduled to retire, he was found dead in bed. One of his business associates remarked: "Mr. Jones forgot to tell God about his plans."

* * *

The law of moderation is apparent in all nature. You need the sun, but if you get too much sun, you suffer sunstroke or heat prostration. You need rain, but too much rain causes flood. You need food, but too much food causes discomfort and an unbalanced physical condition. You need money, but too much money causes all kinds of trouble. It can ruin perfectly good children; it can cause a rift between husband and wife; it can separate good friends. It can cause breakdowns.

Earning a living is a necessary and desirable thing for man. But the making of money is only one part of living. It is by no means all of life. Nor does the ability to amass money deserve the high place in life often accorded it.

* * *

Can you believe in your heart that the money standard which is acceptable to so many so-called successful men is also acceptable to God? Was it for such a goal that He made America and blessed it as no other land has been blessed? Was it for such a standard that Washington and his men fought seven terrible years? Let Washington himself answer: "Providence must have laid some new responsibility upon the people to whom it has given such grandeur and hope." Was it for such a standard that millions of Americans since

Washington's day have risked lives in battle for their country?

* * *

Fulton Oursler wrote: "Among my friends were many who had achieved fame and riches, or, at least, a lot of money in the bank. But no matter how much more wealth they piled up, how often their pictures were on the front page, their new possessions, their new lives—nothing was ever enough. After they got what they wanted, they didn't want it. Without avail, they haunted doctors, and psychiatrists and yogis." Why? Because the world they lived in was the world of self. "A world," continued Oursler, "of self-pity, self-justification, alibis, envies, jealousies, greeds, fears, resentments, grudges and hatreds." Are these things worth while? Do they spell happiness? No, they spell ulcers, breakdowns, premature death. They tell why one person in ten in America has had some mental breakdown at one time or another. All this is the result of self trying to live alone.

* * *

When you ascribe to money supreme and controlling power in your life, you rank it ahead of God. You may hold to God for your "religion," but for all other matters you have made money your God. God gets from you only formal recognition; it is money that calls the signals. In the face of money's great power, you lose all vision and fail to recognize God's Presence within you.

You come to believe you were born into a huge

industrial spider web that holds you fast and keeps you on a treadmill. You feel forced to desert your Partner, the God of Love, for money, the god of torture. You know what is going on and yet you are too weak to do anything about it. Everyone else about you is doing the same thing and you are swept along with the crowd. You should benefit from the advice Rudyard Kipling gave to college students on life's true values:

"Sooner or later, you will see some man to whom the idea of wealth as mere wealth does not appeal, whom the methods of amassing that wealth do not interest, and who will not accept money if you offer it to him at a certain price.

"At first you will be inclined to laugh at this man and to think that he is not 'smart' in his ideas. I suggest that you watch him closely, for he will presently demonstrate to you that money dominates everybody except the man who does not want money. You may meet that man on your farm, in your village, or in your legislature. But be sure that, whenever or wherever you meet him, as soon as it comes to a direct issue between you, his little finger will be thicker than your loins."

To be delivered from the snares and entanglements born of man's economic system, you have only to turn things over to your Partner. Look about you and you will see the simple truth that Mammon's laws do not work. God's laws do. He has provided enough of everything for all His children. If you do your part, your share will come to you. He is generous in His pay. He is not one to stint.

When you become God's agent and co-worker, you will have fun while all the things you really need surely come to you. They may come in the most unexpected ways. A knotty financial problem may find its solution in some trifling incident, a casual remark or meeting someone on the street. What may seem like chance is actually part of your Partner's way of doing things. Put your trust in Him, and concern and fear about money matters will be banished. If you wish to be freed from the monotonous round of the treadmill, pursuing man's standard of success, you know the way. Breathe out ego, breathe in God. Keep practicing this simple natural way of remembering your Partner's Presence. Money will lose its importance to you. Your Partner will open doors where you saw only blank walls.

You may desire money so that you may do good with it, helping others. If so, you need not pursue it; it will come to you. Your Partner is continually seeking those who would be stewards of wealth, not owners. But you must search your heart earnestly. Is your first desire to help others, or is it to gain recognition and popularity for helping others? Ego's ways are subtle. What are you doing with what you now have? Are you helping others? Or is it only with the extra wealth you are seeking that you plan to help others? If you are not doing good with the little you have, the more money you get the more selfish you will become; whatever good you appear to be doing is with the purpose of being lauded and publicly praised.

But there is no need to wait upon wealth to help others. The man who sincerely desires to do good does not wait for his ship to come in; he lovingly approaches the altar of sacrifice, leaves there his gift unnoticed, and departs with a rejoicing heart.

So practice unceasingly the breathing out of your little self, the breathing in of your Higher Self. Practice it again and again and again. Fear about money affairs will leave you. All pressure and strain will depart. In their place will come a calm assurance. Following this will come action based on deep confidence and faith in God—action that will be guided every step of the way by your Partner.

(*These were some of the rebukes that came to me from my Partner.*)

THE LIFE

The New True You

Now that the *truth* had been forced upon me and the *way* shown me, how about the *life?*

After forty years of deluding myself that I stood alone, the *truth* of the Partnership Life had been hammered home by personal experiences in the workaday world. Then I learned that breathing out ego, breathing in God, was the *way* to keep mindful of my Partner's presence. And finally He let it be known that He expected of me a different *life.* "There must be a new you," He said, "the true you."

To be made over sounded like a large order. Moreover, it seemed to have a "religious" connotation, and I wasn't sure I liked that. My Partner soon set me straight: "Nothing pious or sanctimonious is expected of you. You are to be your natural self and not to try to follow in someone else's steps. If you wait upon My guidance and refuse to let ego block the way, a great change will take place in you. This change will continue with each passing day, though not without its ups and downs. You are to keep an open mind, which means you are never to stop learning. I, your Partner, can speak to you in many ways, some not often recognized: through the natural and unaffected ways of children, through men who work with their hands, through wise men and good books, through the noble and ignoble deeds of men, including your own. Danger comes when you stop learning, for then you have stopped seeking my guidance. Study Lincoln. He was always striving to learn "what God was driving at." Following Christ's way, he took no important step without consulting Me, and he entertained no doubts that I really do converse with My children. By now you should know the truth of this. By keeping your mind ever open to My guidance you will re-learn many old truths, among them, these:

* * *

You learn never to take yourself too seriously, knowing in your heart you are but a breath in God's sphere, a leaf in God's forest, a drop in God's ocean.

* * *

You learn that the struggle to keep ego out of the driver's seat is never-ending. Eternal vigilance is the price of the freedom that comes from knowing the truth.

* * *

You learn to let your Partner move your lips and direct your speech, rather than for you yourself to plan in advance what you shall say.

* * *

You learn that the thing you are now engaged in is what counts. "Yesterday is but today's memory, and tomorrow is today's dream."

* * *

You learn you are whole when you are one with

your Partner. When you strive to give of yourself, all is well. It is in your longing to be your Partner's servant that you walk toward true greatness.

* * *

You learn that a better sermon can be preached by your life than by your lips.

* * *

You learn never to remember a benefit you confer, never to forget one conferred upon you.

* * *

You learn the greater the man, the more humbly he regards his part in his Partnership.

* * *

You learn the only conquest that leaves no regrets is conquest over self.

* * *

You learn that love fills the need it finds, and finds the need it fills.

* * *

You learn that when your own little personal world gives signs of breaking up, you need only to breathe out ego, and God fills you with His peace and strength.

* * *

You learn that just as your Partner provides for your growth, so does He provide for your pruning.

* * *

You learn that not only is God in your heart, you are in the heart of God.

You learn to have no other urgent desire than to fulfill your part of the partnership.

* * *

You learn to regard your children not as *your children,* but as children of your Partner, the Creator, who has entrusted them to your care and love. Your greatest responsibility is to give them understanding of their own partnership with their Maker. You may not bequeath your wisdom, but you can pass on to them your faith, your vision and your loving kindness.

* * *

You learn to give yourself with every gift you make. Not to give little of that which you have in abundance. Never to give for the sake of recognition. It is well to give when asked, but better to give unasked. You learn to be grateful for the ability to give, and to strive to make yourself worthy as an instrument of giving.

* * *

You learn that work is not a misfortune or a burden but part of your Partner's plan to give you an active part in your partnership with Him. Work is empty and a curse only when there is no love. For real work is love made visible.

* * *

You learn to beware of the lust for comfort, "that stealthy thing that enters the house as a guest, and then becomes a host, and then a master."

You learn that in passing on to others the things your Partner has passed on to you there is both abundance and joy for you.

* * *

You learn no longer to look forward or backward with fear or even with hope, but to strive only to be a good instrument for your Partner *at this moment.*

* * *

You learn that the poor person is not he who has little but he who wants more.

* * *

You learn that the winter of your discontent soon passes away, and that it has added to your appreciation of the warmth, light and healing power of your Partner.

* * *

You learn that when you forget self and keep your mind on your Partner, He keeps you in perfect peace.

* * *

You learn to become a good listener, for often where it is least expected the voice of your Partner comes through to you.

* * *

You learn not to judge men by their failures, or by their smallest deeds, but only by their heart's desire to work their partnership with God.

* * *

You learn not to judge men by their knowledge or

wisdom, for there is something much greater than
these, understanding of the partnership of man and
Maker. Without this understanding, life has no meaning.

* * *

You learn that in whatever place you find yourself,
it is not your place alone, but His who set you there.

* * *

You learn to see God in everything, making all of
life a great adventure. You see Him playing with your
children, and with their children. You see Him drifting with the clouds, outstretching His arms in the
lightning, descending upon you in the rain. You see
Him in every human being, transcending the super-
ficial ugliness of egotism.

* * *

You learn that only by working with your Partner
are you able to do the thing you have to do when it
ought to be done, whether you like it or not.

* * *

You learn to start wherever you are, with what you
have, and to make something of it.

* * *

You learn the art of consent—to consent to whatever
your Partner deals out to you but never to be satisfied with your own achievements.

* * *

You learn that your happiness depends entirely up-

on whether or not you are working your partnership
with your Maker.

* * *

You learn to depend on your Partnership, not on the
weather, or on fortune or on persons. Your Partner
often may not gratify your immediate wishes, but he
never fails you in any real emergency when you leave
all to Him.

* * *

You learn if you are hidden in an obscure post where
chances of advancement are not bright, never to quit
trying to make yourself a channel through which your
Partner can work. God has a place and a purpose for
every person.

* * *

You learn that it is your Partner who gives you the
strength to act; therefore you try to serve Him in all
your actions. When you cannot feel His presence with
you, your heart knows neither rest nor respite, and
your work becomes endless toil.

* * *

You learn that to try to go through life alone is as
foolish as trying to carry yourself on your own shoul-
ders or coming to beg at your own door. Without your
Partner you are very far from being a whole person.
Let ego go and let God take over. Leave your burdens
on Him who can bear all, and you will never look
back in regret.

* * *

You learn that there are days when the time does

not come true, the words are not properly put end to
end, and the agony of wishing in your heart will not
be stilled. Your desires are many and your eagerness
pitiful, but your Partner will save you by hard refusals.
This is part of your growth toward oneness with your
Partner.

* * *

You learn that there are times when your Partner
seems cruelly to hide Himself from you. His one
purpose is to have you grow and become worthy. He
acts thus to save you from periods of weak, uncertain
desire.

* * *

You learn that nothing is as difficult to take as success. When success comes early in life, it is almost
impossible to take. Unless you know that the only true
wealth is within, you have not the heart to sweep away
the tinsel with which success fills your house.

* * *

You learn that day by day your Partner is making
you worthy of the blessings He gives you, unasked,—
the blue sky and warm sunlight, life, friends, family,
the ability to think clearly.

* * *

You learn that there are times when you want
nothing more than to close your eyes for a while and
rest. You will not force your flagging spirit. Rather
you will give yourself up to this brief rest without a
struggle, putting your whole trust in your Partner,

breathing out ego, breathing in God. In your search for assurance of your Partner's Presence, you learn that only the burning fire of your desire for Him will kindle the Light.

* * *

You learn that there are days when you find it almost impossible to breathe ego out. You would give your whole heart to your Partner, but ego will not let go. It follows wherever you go. Ego adds its loud voice to every word you utter. It knows no shame, but you are ashamed to approach your Partner in such company. But even when you fail to keep Him in your heart's remembrance, His love for you constantly awaits your return.

* * *

You learn that your Partner will give you the strength and poise to bear your joys and sorrows lightly; to make your love fruitful in service; never to disown the poor or bend the knee before mortal might, but rather to raise your mind high above daily trifles and lovingly to surrender your strength to His will.

* * *

You learn that any desire which distracts you from your Partner is false or hollow. When desires or ambitions cloud your mind with delusions and dust, ask your Partner to come with His Light, and if need be with His thunder.

* * *

You learn that the Creator has taken you as Partner in all His wealth. In your heart is the endless play of His delight; in your life His will is ever taking shape. To captivate your heart, your Partner has decked all nature in beauty.

* * *

You learn that you may idle now and then and grieve over lost time, but time with your Partner is never lost. He has taken every moment of your life into His hands. Hidden in the heart of things, He nourishes seeds into sprouts, buds into blossoms and flowers into fruit.

* * *

You learn that when you bring sorrow to your Partner as an offering of faith and trust, He rewards you with His grace. His love eases the pain in your heart and changes sorrow to joy.

* * *

You learn that the Partnership Life is no "pasteboard religion," no sentimental cult. It is God's truth. It is His plan. It stands as the rock upon which all true religion is founded.

* * *

You learn that just as your body rallies to mend a hurt or to drive out a foreign invader, so does your Father's world rally to repel anyone who would harm it. The Creator who made your body also made the universe, and it is He who sustains both.

* * *

You learn that the universe works toward wholeness. It is thoroughly honest, returning measure for measure what is put into it.

* * *

You learn to think of your Partner as Spirit and as Light, an invisible Light within you. This Light is not an organ like the heart or lungs yet it gives life to and controls the organs. The Light is not a faculty like the ability to remember, to figure, to compare, but it uses these as hands and feet. It is not the intellect or the will, but the Master of them both. It is the foundation of your being. It shines through you upon things and makes you aware that you are nothing and that the Light is all.

* * *

You learn that when you let the Light work through you, divine wisdom enters your heart and mind. Old things pass away, and with them all cares. Joy, achievement, love and power flow through you. The Light is of the Creator, and He is all powerful, all wise, all loving. Whoever opposes the Creator's Will is sooner or later balked and baffled; that is the Law. Could there be a greater miracle than God imparting His own Spirit to His human child? Could there be a greater gift than God's gift of Himself to every man and woman He creates? The Light within is this gift.

* * *

You learn that when you would be something of yourself, you weaken your will and intellect and soon are lost and drifting. The Light must be given its way to flow through every part of you and to heal and love and guide you. The Light was there before the ego appeared. It will continue after the ego has gone. The Light will make you as a person immortal, but only if you let it rule your life. Then everyone will see not you but the Light. Men are starving for the Light. They will give all they have for what they see in an illuminated man.

* * *

You learn that when you let the Light guide you, concern over things like money, ambition, fame, and your condition in the world disappears. The world itself loses its false importance. Only the Light counts. And the law of the Light is as perfect as the laws that govern chemistry, astronomy and the growth of fruit and flowers. This realization loosens materialism's grip upon you.

* * *

You learn that the Light within possesses an essential wisdom far greater than any acquired wisdom. Whatever may be new to you is already well known to the Light. Its justice is perfect, its viewpoint is universal, and its love extends to all. It looks to the Light in every human being. All you need do is to get out of its way and let it shine. Until you do this, you go from bad to worse. Worldly men may deem you successful, but without the Light you are only a shell full of the pride of self. Without a heart rich in love, a wealthy man is a miserable beggar. Only the Light can teach. The ego cannot teach. It only babbles. But when you get your self out of the way, the Light pours its wisdom through you, opening the door to love, courage and all the virtues.

* * *

You learn that to admit the primacy of the Light is not to deny the existence of worldly things. It is only to recognize that all things are expressions of the Light and completely under its control. The Light has the power. It is the Creator. The Light within you is not subject to your will. You can do nothing to violate its serenity. You cannot disturb God.

* * *

You learn that the Light does not keep itself aloof in a pious, sanctimonious manner. It is the primal goodness, seeking to work through you, inviting you to grow in sweetness and in joy. The Light makes for unbelievable happiness.

* * *

You learn to let your Partner write for you in even so common a matter as a letter. Every writer knows himself to be a man of moods. He knows, too, that these moods often do not believe in each other. One day he is full of thoughts and can express himself easily and clearly. The next day he faces a dreary dearth of ideas and words. He wonders who it was that wrote so freely yesterday. The answer is simple: Yesterday he was a channel, and His Partner was able to flow ideas through him. Today there is no channel. Unwittingly, perhaps through lack of understanding or appreciation, self has blocked the way and the Creative Spirit cannot reach him. The block may have a physical or a mental or moral cause, but the result in any case is to lose contact with the Author of all good ideas.

When self takes over the driver's seat, the Creative Spirit abdicates. This freedom has been given to you. When you exercise your right to take over, however, you find yourself struggling ineffectually to put the proper thought and words together. It will always be so. When you find yourself thus frustrated, a quiet time is in order, a time to meet with your Partner and to listen in silence for His guidance. You will soon regain your proper place as channel.

* * *

You learn a basic truth always known to true artists: Nothing worthwhile is done *by* man; it is done *through* him. Man can be a god in nature, or he can be a weed by the wall. Let him choose as his ruler between self and the Creative Spirit of God. Both inhabit him. Both are necessary to the partnership, the one to guide and inspire, the other to follow and work. It is an unbeatable team when it works that way. The trouble starts when one's pride insidiously coaxes self to take over. "You are great," it says admiringly. "People are singing your praises." And indeed maybe they are, but you should know in your heart to whom the credit belongs, even if your admirers don't have that understanding. Knowledge of your Partner's working through you insures humility. One cannot possibly practice the Partnership Life and not be humble. The praise of the world cannot fool such a man. Worldly honor cannot tempt him to "sell the thrones of angels for a short and turbulent pleasure." To forsake the blessed Spirit for the fickle and false plaudits of men is unthinkable to him.

* * *

You learn that the things that belong to you somehow will gravitate to you. They need not be pursued with strain and worry.

* * *

You learn that the presence within you of the Creative Spirit is not a theory or a pious hope but a fact to be experienced. When the waves of God's Spirit flow into you, they confer upon you a greatness and an ecstasy that are indescribable. For their duration, you share the Creator's majesty, power and love.

* * *

You learn with a deep sense of gratitude that when self abdicates in favor of God, you do not grow old but grow young. When you realize the truth of your partnership with God, your eyes are uplifted, your wrinkles are smoothed, you are inspired with hope and power.

* * *

You learn not to lament your lack of special talents. As long as you have God you have character, and character contributes more to those about you than does talent. Seeing character in you, people take heart from the ease and simplicity with which your difficulties are handled, and they face their own with greater confidence and understanding.

* * *

You learn about the cell which reproduces other cells and keeps on reproducing. Happiness is that kind of cell. Love is that kind of cell. Try to keep happiness and love for yourself and there is no multiplication, so they die. It is the law. Give the cells of happiness and love to others, and they start multiplying so rapidly you cannot keep track of them, and a good deal of this reproduction comes back to you. Again it is the law. It cannot be otherwise. That is the Maker's plan. You cannot love or be happy by yourself or for yourself alone.

* * *

You learn to stop in the park or in the woods and to look at the soft shades in the sky, the lush greens of the summer trees, the brilliant colors in the Fall. And you learn to see the great loving Hand responsible for it all. With what serenity and spontaneity God works. The complete absence of pressure and tension. How He permits century to follow century while He perfects a wildflower. The miracles that are accomplished when man gets out of God's way! Then you resolve that you will not let men run your life for you. You will no longer be forced to go down the wrong road, until sickness from strain or worry brings on early death. You will live the life your Maker intended. This may mean taking up by the roots and transplanting elsewhere. It may merely mean a change of heart and belief. But you will no longer live alone, no longer follow the stupid dictates of self. True freedom is yours only when you have broken the chains with which self binds you in slavery.

* * *

You learn that you cannot separate your faith from your action; your belief from your occupation. You cannot divide your hours, allotting so many to God, the rest to yourself. Your day-to-day life is your real religion. "Better be naked than wear morality as your best garment." One does not become a follower of Christ by calling himself a Christian. A Christian is one who believes Christ's saying that "the Kingdom of God is within you" and tries earnestly to practice Christ's way of life.

* * *

You learn not to rail at frustration. Frustration mothers many creations. Out of frustration symphonies have been composed, classics written, noble deeds done. Can you believe that to your Partner there is such a thing as frustration? It is only the closing of a door in order that another door leading to greater things may open for you.

* * *

You learn not to alibi even to yourself that you have inherited certain weaknesses. You have within you a

reservoir of power and strength far greater than all
inherited weaknesses. To call upon it, you need only to
get yourself out of your Partner's way. He is all the
strength and power you need to overcome any weakness.

* * *

You learn, when unjustly accused or held up to
ridicule, to accept the experience as necessary for your
better development, in order that God's purposes may
be more clearly understood and that you may become a
more perfect channel for His power. "Neither hath this
man sinned, nor his parents, but that the works of God
shall be made manifest in him." Viewed in the proper
light, *everything* that happens can bring you closer to
God.

* * *

You learn that you are a stream which cannot rise
higher than its source. If the source of your actions is
self with its mechanistic and materialistic assumption,
your life will take on a false, distorted aspect. If the
source of your actions is your Maker, then all your
thoughts and deeds take on a color of truth and beauty.

* * *

You learn that the best way to help anyone is to
live your Partnership Life. The life you live is a reflection of what you think of your Partner.

* * *

You learn that all is One, and you look within yourself to understand your neighbor, your friend, your

foe. Your attitude toward them is your attitude toward your Creator.

* * *

You learn that lip service and knowledge alone are useless, unless followed by action. To know, and not to act accordingly, is to mock your Partner.

* * *

You learn that every other person has as much right on earth as you. The fact that he may not be as well informed or as well educated doesn't change the right. It is not knowledge that counts, but making yourself a channel for God to work through. College degrees do not necessarily guarantee wisdom. The brilliant mind that is slanted violently in any direction is disqualified to think truly. The world owes much to people who, though not very profound, are guided by the Light and say without effort the thing which has been long wanted and hunted in vain.

* * *

You learn that you are not here by chance. You are here for a purpose, and no one can fulfill that purpose but you. You can fulfill it only by working your partnership with God. If you devote yourself to ways of self-exaltation, you put the false god of self before the true God. This sin defeats the purpose for which you were made: oneness with God.

* * *

You learn that what matters most in your life is not mere belief but actual experience. It was not just belief in Christ or God that knit the early Christians together. It was their own experiences of individual partnership with God. This is not to under-rate the value of ritual and dogma when used to strengthen one's Partnership Life. It is rather to suggest that ritual and dogma should not supplant actual experience of the Kingdom within. Nor should they be permitted to distract from the central purpose of steady communion with God. They should be as an open door, not a barrier, to the Partnership Life.

* * *

You learn that just as the body works spontaneously and naturally to heal its own wounds, so does the universe work to right its own wounds. No one can successfully hurt the universe for long, because it works to right things, and no man or group of men can interfere with the balance which the Creator holds in His hands.

* * *

You learn that "Love your neighbor as yourself" doesn't mean "love your Catholic neighbor as yourself, or your Methodist neighbor, or your Jewish neighbor, or your union neighbor as yourself." The Master said, "Love your neighbor"—whoever or whatever he might be—"as yourself." You grow, you become lovable, you enjoy life and real success only as you follow this commandment.

* * *

You learn that people who hate are sick. They should

be treated—as indeed they will be in some future time—
to help them recover. Sickness is a state of unbalance;
its cause may be physical, mental or spiritual. To restore balance, one must be made whole. He who gave
you life and provided the means to sustain that life
will restore wholeness if His simple laws are obeyed.

* * *

You learn that if you love people and want to help
people, you will not have to hunt them up; they will
hunt you up. If the Light within you is shining, people
will be attracted to it because they need the help you
can give them.

* * *

You learn that there is great joy in being a shepherd. It is a rare joy, for an unusual degree of self-
lessness is required to be a shepherd. In those occasional
moments when in your love for others you are able
to forget self completely and let nothing stand in the
way of helping them, you qualify as a shepherd. This
is a great experience, ennobling, enriching, rewarding.

* * *

You learn that you cannot change people. Your
Partner changes them. Your Partner may work
through you to change people. They will look at you
but see your Partner. Seeing what your Partner has
done for you, they will want that for themselves. So
do not be a "do-gooder" or a reformer. Just play
your part as an instrument for God. He will do the
rest. He stands ready to work miracles through you

just as readily as the genie of Aladdin's Lamp. But instead of rubbing a lamp, man needs to rub himself out of the number one spot. Real miracles are then performed. When anyone praises you for these wonders, do not hesitate to set them straight as to where the credit is due. The Master set you a clear enough example: "Why callest thou me good? There is only one that is good, the Father."

* * *

You learn that when ego is the judge, honesty takes on strange forms. There can be phony kinds of honesty: honesty-where-money-is-concerned, honesty-where examinations-are-concerned, honesty-where-athletics-are-concerned, honesty-where-personal-relations-are-concerned, honesty-where-unimportant-details are concerned. Ego can pretend to any number of separate "honesties."

Many a parent has unfortunately affected the thinking of his own children by his attitude toward these so-called "little sins:" the railroad ticket that isn't collected, accepting without comment a dollar too much change when paying a bill, and other similar "smart" ways of gaining without initiating anything dishonest, may seem harmless to the parent, but the effect on the child is to weaken his moral fibre. Christ had some strong words to say about those who caused "little ones to stumble." Nothing—least of all honesty—can be left safely to ego to decide.

Better that you be left in ignorance as to the true

greatness within you than to know the truth of your partnership with God and not be guided by Him in all things. Lip service and mere intellectual awareness are a dangerous foundation of sand on which to build. Action is the measure and the rock foundation of partnership with God.

* * *

You learn from the naturalness of a child's smile that all the naturally delightful, kindly, gracious things you do, are born of the Higher Will within you. These are the selfless things, acts of kindness and of love that bring joy to others and cause people to love you. Selfish things always spring from the will of ego.

* * *

You learn out of what formerly would have been disappointments, to cultivate patience, the least understood and possibly the most beautiful of all the virtues. In patience, it is God who possesses you. In impatience it is ego. Impatience is a projection of ego into God's affairs.

* * *

You learn that pride is a moral sin, which can affect you physically by actual crippling. Some ailments are said to be caused by frustration.

* * *

You learn that your Partner will help you determine your inner life goal and guide you in attaining it, using the whole of you, with the physical, mental and spiritual parts all integrated. This goal will be of service to God. Success will follow your pursuit of this goal, as "the wheel follows the ox."

* * *

You learn to start where your are, using what is at hand. You become aware of the human tendency to disregard simple, close-at-hand facts when complex and distant ones seem more intriguing. You are reminded that you can use only what you have at hand. A thousand mile journey begins with one step. Others will soon see the Father working in you. Unconsciously you will be encouraging the faint and the weak, giving strength and courage to the faltering.

* * *

You learn, unmindful of what a man's sins may be, to stretch out a hand to help him.

* * *

You learn to refrain from telling your Partner where you would like to work or serve. Your attitude becomes: "Lord, I am yours. Use me as you see fit." Your Partner will help you build with what you have, starting where you are, little by little, line upon line. You will not be in haste or over-anxious, for you know the whole of the building is of His making.

* * *

You learn that a man's true strength, grace, art and wit lie in the presence of God within him. Under his Partner's guidance, the body can carry out the most highly complicated directions with ease. It is when mind and body consent to be guided that things go best. Your Partner's Spirit controls every cell, every muscle, every nerve. When man allows the Creative Spirit free play, he rises to his greatest artistry and genius.

* * *

You learn that the biographer and the psychiatrist of the future will not limit themselves to an examination of a person's outer life or a profile of his personality. The task will be to discover and reveal who was the senior member of that particular Partnership, ego or God.

* * *

You learn that man's real conflicts spring from inner sources; from the struggle between good and evil, between conscience and desire, between reason and passion, between the spirit and the flesh. Christ simplified things for you by establishing that God is within, and that all things work for your good if you submerge your will in His. *You learn* to live this truth. No matter what your difficulty—an unhappy home life, frustrated ambition, loneliness, illness, an inferiority complex—the ultimate solution of your painful situation lies within you. Unblock the way by removing ego as the head man. Breathe ego out of the number one spot. It does not belong there. It did not create you. It does not sustain you. You were created and are sustained by the one Creator. His Creative Spirit was with you from the beginning. It is with you now, integrated with every part of your being. It is your eternal Partner. So breathe out ego, breathe in God.

* * *

You learn that the more you let your Partner run your Partnership, the greater is your peace of mind. Every moment that you work your Partnership is full of joy which at times borders on ecstasy. Life was made for this kind of joy. "My joy I give thee; not as the world knoweth joy." Your Partner is a God of Love, a God of Joy, and it is His pleasure to make your life one of rich happiness if you will let Him. If God is with you, who can be against you? When you see anyone take himself too seriously (it may on occasion happen to you!), it will seem so ridiculous you may burst out laughing.

* * *

You learn not to look too eagerly for results. One does not pull up a growing vegetable from the earth just to make sure it is growing. You plant and water and fertilize and work—and wait. The growth is your Partner's gift. He grants the increase in your stature, in your character and ability to serve, provided you do your share—and patiently wait.

* * *

You learn to do what is good, but not because it pays to do good. You do good because your Partner guides you to see that it is the beautiful, the fitting, the loving and the proper thing, and you do it for the sheer joy of doing it. *You learn* that the Master did not try to make people good. He strove to give people joy.

He knew they could be truly joyous only if they were conscious of the Presence of God within them and let Him work through them. True goodness follows in the wake of true joy.

* * *

You learn never to pity yourself. Gratitude fills your heart when conditions are favorable; consent and faith are yours when things appear to go wrong. *You learn* that "bad" results often are opportunities. You welcome adversity as the "prosperity of the great."

* * *

You learn never to evade or run from a difficult situation. The problem will have to be met sooner or later. Your Partner gives you the necessary strength to meet it now.

* * *

You learn that love is the great creative energy. Love renews and rebuilds you. God is Love. Love is God. Therefore love is your Creative Partner. Latent within you is the perfection that is love. *You learn* to identify yourself with it by making yourself a channel through which love may flow to your neighbor. First breathe out ego, breathe in God; and when the ego is transformed, if only intermittently, into a channel for God, then you can breathe out love to mankind, breathe in God's love for you.

* * *

You learn how badly the world needs laughter— hearty, joyous, barbless laughter. Men's minds are harassed by uncertainty and fear of sudden destruction; the relaxing and healing medicine of laughter reaches to all parts of the body and mind. Laughter is the Creative Spirit bubbling over with joy.

* * *

You learn that the purpose of your Partnership is not to ensure that life will be easy and material success swift. Success is usually coupled with increased authority, and authority over others is always dangerous. When not accompanied by understanding, it is highly dangerous. When not coupled with true humility, it is explosively dangerous. The more authority the greater the danger. The peak is reached in communism and other forms of statism, which resemble the disease of cancer. They breed spiritually blind men who put themselves ahead of the Power that sustains them every moment.

* * *

You learn that when the average person reaches age 33, he begins to decline physically, as shown by statistics of the U. S. Public Health Service. *You learn* that this need not be. You can become younger in body, in mind and spirit. You can feel younger tomorrow, next month, next year, if you will follow your Creative Partner's simple laws. He will make you whole. He will renew your vitality. "They that wait upon the Lord shall renew their strength; they shall mount up with wings as eagles; they shall run, and not be weary; and they shall walk, and not faint."

You learn to re-examine again this thing called "success." You look into what it gives you and what it takes away. It may give you a fat bank account and a false sense of security. But it may also take away your health and the sweetness and love of your family life. It may take away friends and other things of real value. Are you pursuing success for the sake of your family? Perhaps they would rather have you than your success. They'd rather have you spend more time with them than leave them your money. The "success" of ego always has too great a price attached to it. True success bears a tag reading: "Free to him who yields his ego to God."

*   *   *

You learn to keep yourself open to guidance, but you realize that guidance is not inflexible. The particular thing you feel guided to do actually may be done in a manner quite different from what you anticipated. So take it easy and keep listening to others. They may be the means your Partner uses to reach you.

*   *   *

You learn that your Partner often works in mysterious ways to get His wishes to you. Some of these ways may take a long while to be made known to you. During all this time you are growing, so as to be ready for the next step when it is made clear. *You learn* little by little not to confuse what you want to do with what God wants you to do.

*   *   *

You learn that, broadly speaking, people may be divided into three classes, holding the following attitude toward God:

1. There is no God. Life is the result of unplanned evolutions.
2. There is a God, but He stands aloof and allows man to work things out for himself.
3. God is a Spirit, integrated within every human being.

To the first class, this can be said: Scientists now insist that too many things happen too regularly and dependably for life to be the result of unplanned evolutions. There is a plan to life, and so there must be a Planner.

The second class includes most people in America today. They believe in a God that created the earth, left it to man to run, and waits now to judge each man as he passes from earth.

Of the third class, Christ is the leader. "The Kingdom of God is within you. . . I speak not from myself, but the Father abiding in me, He doeth the works. He telleth me what to say. . . The things I do, you too can do." Christ proclaimed God's presence in man and then went on to prove it by the way He lived. The early Christians followed His way of life, as do true Christians to this day.

* * *

You learn that education which does not promote understanding of the Partnership of man and Maker is futile. Christ opposed the church of his day because it was satisfied to go through the motions of faith in God. The Master taught that God is within each human being, eager to bring joy, love, achievement and inner peace, if only man will let Him work through him. To follow Christ's way of life, all phases of living must be integrated with God as the fountainhead. The child will then know for a certainty that he does not stand alone. He will know that he has for a permanent Partner the Creator of the Universe.

* * *

You learn that the devil has his point of contact within your ego, for his whole appeal is always to your lower self. He works in countless ways and exists in countless forms. Whenever you are filled with the glow of self-satisfaction, the devil breathes and flourishes in your ego. Breathe him out and breathe God in. Every time you speak a thoughtless word, failing to see within your fellow-man the same Creative Spirit that is within you, the devil's work in the world is prospered. Every time some form of escapism diverts you from your appointed task, the devil in your ego has won another victory. You cause him to vanish when you breathe out ego, breathe in God.

* * *

You learn always to be on guard, for never is ego more dangerous than when it induces you to feel pride in your nearness to God. Ego's most subtle weapon is pride, and sometimes pride in your own humility. This is unconsciously to appropriate credit which belongs only to your Partner; the devil in your ego knows this, and loves it. He is forever looking for some new corner in your make-up where he may conceal himself. Discover him there, and he laughs you to scorn while seeking yet another hide-out.

But there is a way to outwit the devil: Breathe out ego with every outgoing breath. Take time to do the job right. Go off by yourself, practicing breathing out ego while you ask for God's forgiveness. You will receive it with each incoming breath.

* * *

You learn that every channel eventually empties into a larger body of water; that even the largest ocean is fed by tiny individual drops of rainwater, each drop having yielded its individuality to join with other drops to achieve its destiny.

The next time you are assailed by frustration, ponder a moment on the ways of a channel. *You learn* from it one of the greatest lessons of life, to yield spontaneously and completely, without fears or inhibitions, to the Creative Spirit which gave you life and sustains you each moment. Everything works for good for those who trust and surrender to this great and loving force. He who loses his life shall find it. He who is willing to be last shall be first. This is the Partnership Life that Christ came to establish. It is not just for an hour on a Sunday morning, not just for special occasions when man prays because he needs something. It is an eternal Partnership in all things at all times.

You learn that in the workaday world the tendency is to see only the material aspect of life, and this one-sided approach begets disaster. Life in reality is one. There is an invisible spiritual aspect as well as a visible material aspect of the same life. The spiritual and the material are inextricably one, infused with one another, known in and through each other. When man knows himself to be indivisibly united with his Creator, he then knows that the whole purpose of life is to realize and express this oneness with God.

* * *

You learn to look for God in every person you meet. You see the true man clear through the physical man. You feel the underlying unity of all in God. Therefore you meet people on the plane of their highest abilities and noblest capacities. By this very act, you promote the best in them and help make it their normal way. Their gratitude and love strengthen your own faith.

* * *

You learn to work with a song in your heart. You are in love with life. Ever conscious of your Partner's Presence, you see Him everywhere. Little worries no longer are stumbling blocks to you, but stepping stones to God.

* * *

You learn that prayer is the practice of the Presence of God: the Partnership in action. Communion with God, yes, and more; prayer is the soul's sincere desire to be a perfect channel for God. Prayer is feeling: "I am nothing, God is everything." True prayer goes beyond asking for things, even beyond interceding for a loved one. God knows your needs before you ask. He knows your friend's needs, too. Prayer should not tell God how to run His business.

Prayer is not like a window, to open and to shut. True prayer is steady and constant communion. Prayer is your heart saying to God, "In giving me more of Thyself, Thou givest all."

* * *

You learn that the Golden Rule is not enough. When a man says, "My religion is the Golden Rule," he means well, but is he not relying on self to the exclusion of his Higher Self? If he is good already, think what a team he would make working with his eternal creative Partner. Nothing would be impossible for him. He would appear to men as one with Light coming out of him. Would it not be a pity for him to rest content on the Golden Rule? It could easily lull him into ignorance of his real destiny. But if he recognized his Partnership, the Golden Rule would follow as fruit follows the blossom. Very much more would also follow as by-products of the Partnership: courage, integrity, loyalty, devotion, compassion, humility and all other noble qualities.

* * *

You learn that there is an area where the chances of finding material security are greatest. This is the area of moderation. When a man goes beyond it, he loses security. The Creator has established a law which says, "Too much of anything is not good for man."

When anyone begins to accumulate too much money, his perspective becomes warped. His whole viewpoint becomes tinged with the color of money. He gets to worrying about his possessions and about the possibility of losing them. He worries about high taxes; he begins to hate anyone who threatens to interfere with his plans to accumulate still more wealth or to hold on to what he has. He loses the joy that a small amount of money used to bring him. Now a thousand times as much fails to yield him real satisfaction.

Security is not a state of finances. It is a state of mind. You may possess much, but if you feel insecure, you *are* insecure. Insecurity can come from having too much as well as from having too little. The way to real security is to let your Creative Partner take over. "Put thine hand into the hand of God. That shall be to thee better than light and safer than a known way."

* * *

You learn that there is no such thing as an invention. Discoveries, yes. Inventions, no. All of what man calls inventions have been prepared for him in advance by the Creative Power. The necessary materials were placed here so that man would have the fun of working with them and discovering wonderful combinations of them. Is not the Creator saying to you: "Here is the earth, rich with minerals and other elements.

Here is something to excite your interest and your talents. Work with these things in your laboratories. You will discover some wonderful things, some that are useful and, if you choose, some that are destructive. But there are two things you must not tamper with: (1) the creation of life, (2) the sustaining of life. These two are Mine. And regarding these I am a jealous God, jealous to save My children from pain and disease and untimely death.

"I created life, and I have supplied all the elements necessary to sustain life. These are My secrets. Let man study them if he will, but let him not interfere with My processes of creating and sustaining life. In the foods of the earth, in the waters that spring from the earth, in the healing rays of the sun, in the air which carries My Presence into the very heart and being of man, I have placed the life-giving elements necessary to replenish man from day to day. Your scientists now know that when man removes from My natural foods the life-giving elements I have placed there in ways man can never imitate, he seriously impairs his health and shortens his life."

* * *

You learn to look beyond mere outward seeming into the reality that is within. You know the folly of trying to judge a person by his appearance. Who would identify Ghandi by his looks as one of the greatest souls of modern times? Who would identify Lincoln by sight as one of the greatest Americans, if not the greatest?

Christ saw beyond the appearance of men into their hearts and souls. In the light of this He could not hate anyone. It would be like hating God, for God made each person and He took up his abode within each. Christ loved even the worst sinners because He saw their Creative Partner within them. Loving them, He helped them to renewed faith in themselves.

As you begin to experience real love for people, you sense deep within yourself an inexplicable, expanding feeling of warmth. It is the Master's promise come true. It is the divine joy in fulfilling the divine commandment to love one another.

* * *

You learn to consent readily when your Partner throws a stop light on your plans. Your faith in Him grows with observation and an open mind. You wait for guidance and the green light. No longer do you set your own time limit for events. You are content to leave this to your Partner. You trust His guidance. Observe the birds as they dart at such speed through the air. What keeps them from colliding? It is their complete obedience to guidance. Smart and intelligent human animals bump into one another at street corners, in automobiles, in trains, even in planes. Somehow they continue to feel sure they know where they are going.

* * *

You learn to pause, even in the midst of urgent matters, to give your Creative Partner a chance to get

His thoughts to you. In a conference when the atmosphere has grown heated or tense, you quietly say
to yourself, "Let's take a minute off to listen to what
our Partner may be trying to get over to us." In the
space of a minute or so, by breathing self out and
breathing God in, you are filled with peace of mind
and given the right answer, both at the same time.
Many hard-headed, practical, successful men work
this way. They know that the right answers are not
figured out *by* them. They come *through* them.

So be quiet every now and then and let the Senior
Partner get through to you. He is within you and
knows all the answers, but of course if you do not
unblock His way by getting out of the number one
spot, He cannot get the answers to you. In order to
tune in, you must first tune yourself out. Breathe out
ego, breathe in God. You'll soon be on the beam. Coun-
sel, guidance and a beautiful peace of mind come flooding in. You feel physically strengthened. The invigorating effect is like that of mountain air. Thus you learn
to use the quiet time and the simple technique of breathing in God's love as regular practice.

* * *

You learn all the well-known admonitions, "Be good,
be kind, be brave," are not really to the point. One
thing only is needed, to keep your ego out of God's
way. God, your Partner, is always good and kind and
brave and everything that is virtuous. He waits at
your door and knocks. You need only to bid Him enter and take over. Life is simple when you let Him

guide you. This truth is known to babes. Why should it be hidden from wise men?

* * *

You learn that the end of man is not the Almighty State, as communistic and similar ideologies hold. And man himself is not the end of man, as in the humanist view. The end of man is oneness with his Maker. For that he was born. Toward that end he must strive. Only then does he know joy, power, love and peace of mind. In no other way can he fulfill his destiny. The prophets said it. Every great man has said it. The greatest of all men proved it by His life.

* * *

You learn that children possess naturally certain lovely arts which adults have lost. There are at least three things at which a child is a genius and which enrich your own life when you recapture them:

1. A child can listen. Watch him while he is hearing a fairy tale. He listens with his whole being. When adults listen, their minds often are miles away or waiting to speak their own thoughts.
2. The child can be delighted. What is a lovelier picture than a happy child, innocent eyes shining with the light of his eternal Creative Partner? Adults delight in fleeting escapisms.
3. The child can trust. His faith in his Partner is complete. He sleeps peacefully wherever he is put. He entrusts himself fully to the Power that

gave him life, with never a thought that this Power might not sustain him. Adults, harassed on all sides by the pressures of a materialistic world, do not know whom, or what, to trust.

The Partnership life restores your viewpoint to that of the child you really are.

* * *

You learn the fallacy of the common belief that what happens to you comes from outside yourself, that you are at the mercy of heredity, circumstances and environment. Placing your faith in your Partner within, you no longer depend on outside things for support or comfort. It used to be that your spirits would rise with some favorable event—a victory in politics or sports, an increase in stock market values, a recovery from sickness, the return of a close friend —but now you begin to know better. You realize that nothing can bring you peace but your Partner. By keeping your eye single to His Presence, your whole body is filled with Light.

* * *

You learn that you cannot fear that which you love, and when you see your loving Partner in all things, your faith in His way grows sure and unshakable. You come to see that everything that happens to you —the so-called good and the so-called bad—have one purpose, to bring you into closer unity with the great Creative Spirit.

You learn to stand up for the other fellow's rights, but not for your own. Fighting for your own rights is a blind alley. Nearly always it is your ego claiming its "rights."

* * *

You learn that your Partner's healing intelligence within you works steadily to keep you strong and in good repair. Observe how He acts to heal every cut and bruise your body may suffer. Without delay He sets in motion all the forces needed to mend the damage. He requires little of you, only that you do not interfere with His healing processes.

* * *

You learn not to judge men who live without understanding of the Partnership life. You will meet more than one man who will cause you to say to yourself, shame-facedly, "I was once like that—and in unguarded moments I am still like that—so sure of myself, so oblivious of the presence of a Higher Power within me."

* * *

You learn that no matter how brilliantly a man speaks, if he is not being inspired by a source greater than himself, he cannot inspire others to worthy and noble deeds.

* * *

You learn that "God helps those who help themselves" is better read "God helps those who help others." An even better version may be "God helps those who humble themselves." Christ promised that the meek shall inherit the earth. *You learn* how accurate this is as regards the earth's true values. Of course you do not sit back and leave everything to your Partner. Your vital function in the Partnership is to develop and make use of your God-given talents. If you fail in your part, the particular thing which you were created to do will never be done. *No one knows what powers lie dormant in the secret storerooms of his mind.* Only by unblocking the way for your Partner can you bring these gifts into view.

* * *

You learn that your Divine Partner is always pressing upon you, as the sun presses upon a room when the shades are drawn. Raise the shades and the room is flooded with sunlight. Remove ego and your heart is flooded with the love and power and peace of your Partner. "Eye hath not seen, nor ear heard, neither hath entered into the heart of man, the things which God hath prepared for them that love Him."

* * *

You learn never to make a decision, even a minor one, when ego is in the saddle.

* * *

You learn to admire and appreciate beautiful works without desiring to possess them. This does not exclude beautiful women, nor, for the gentler sex, strong, personable men.

* * *

You learn that the Light within you is like a sunbeam. It cannot really be hidden. You may step on a sunbeam to cover it, but the beam comes out on top. The Light within you cannot permanently be darkened. It will shine through every effort to obscure it, for it is the Eternal Light.

* * *

You learn that even when you go wrong, your Partner comes to your aid and comfort. He knows you and knows that error is a part of your make-up. But do not expect that He will save you from embarrassment if you are still holding on to personal pride. He has not covenanted with you that you should never appear to disadvantage. Sometimes you may even cut a ridiculous figure. Everyone needs such humbling. If you were not too concerned with the opinion of others, you would not be hurt. The true man is never hurt, only the ego.

Ego has its taproot in pride. C. S. Lewis wrote: "Pride leads to every other vice; it is the complete anti-God state of mind." Pride disregards the Creator's part in your everyday life, because it denies the Partnership of man and Maker. Faith in your Partnership with God begets humility. "The first test of a truly great man," wrote John Ruskin, "is his humility. I do not mean by humility doubt of his own power. But really great men have a curious feeling that this greatness is not *in* them but *through* them. And they see something divine in every other man, and are endlessly, foolishly, incredibly merciful."

You learn that growth occurs only where there is humility; it is arrested in the presence of pride. When the ego is inflated with self-importance, the Author of all good works is ignored. Pride puts a shutter on the mind. It corrupts the conscience and spoils whatever virtues one possesses.

Know yourself and you cannot be proud. When you breathe out ego, breathe in God, you remind yourself that everything you have has been given you and that your Partner is the Giver. And so you are filled with a deep and abiding sense of gratitude.

* * *

You learn the truth of the old proverb: "God bestows his gifts during the night." For while you sleep, your Partner is working in your behalf. He is busy digesting the food you recently enjoyed eating. While you are resting, His clouds are storing supplies of moisture for your needs. In the earth seeds are swelling. In the fields He is ripening grain for you. On the trees fruits are being made ready for you. In the mellow darkness of the night, God is preparing this precious harvest.

These miracles are performed without the aid of your restless activity. This is not to belittle the part you play or the work you do but to remind you that God never rests in His devotion to you. He always provides the increase. So breathe out ego, breathe in God. Your Partner is saying to you: "I want to work through you. I want to fill you with joy. I have need

of you. Be My agent and instrument. Let us work together. I want to do great things through you."

* * *

You learn that the source of all trouble lies within
the ego. You may not like to believe this, but you will
find that it is true. *No matter what your problem,* you
need only to get the ego out of the way and your Partner will make the solution clear to you. The problem
may not go away. Its disappearance might be the
worst thing that could happen to you. The difficulty
may remain, but your attitude toward it will be different. Your confidence in your Partner will be such
that you leave the problem completely in His hands.
Therein lies the real solution.

Sooner or later every spiritually unprepared person
is faced with a situation that cannot be met by self
alone. A great crisis thrusts itself upon him. Then it
is late to learn the practice of breathing out ego, breathing in God.

The time to get ready spiritually is now. The wisdom of prevention rather than cure applies here more
than anywhere. The way to handle every problem that
may confront you in life is to breathe out ego, breathe
in God. By doing this now and keeping at it, you will
be prepared for any eventuality.

* * *

You learn that one way to make your Partnership
Life effective is to undertake something so great that

it cannot be accomplished without the help of your
Partner.

* * *

You learn that one way in which your Partner
helps you overcome the fear of advancing old age or
of being alone is by getting you to do something for
others, particularly for those unable to do things for
themselves. In helping them you rid yourself of fears.
You need do nothing outstanding or sensational to
make others happy. "A good man out of the good
treasure of the heart bringeth forth good things." *You
learn* to make a hobby of helping others, if it's nothing
more than seeing shut-ins. You yourself come away
helped and blessed.

* * *

You learn that your Partner often will save you
from impatience, that little eager beaver who cannot
wait for things to ripen. And God will screen from
you premature ideas. Under the Partnership, your
eyes cannot see opportunities staring you in the face
until you have ripened and are ready for them. Then
you notice them, and the period when you were blind
to them seems a strange dream.

* * *

You learn that material resources are depleted with
use, but the more you use spiritual resources the greater they become. You grow as they grow. You grow
nearer to your Maker and to your fellow-man.

You learn not to stop with dreaming. God working through you makes you a doer. Being a dreamer is important. Every achievement was first a dream or an idea. But to transform an idea into reality, action is necessary. To make that action right, *you learn* to get out of God's way and become his hands and feet. That is your part of the Partnership. You do not sit back and wait for things to happen.

You get your joy in being busy, following your Partner's guidance. It is your part to weed and work the land. It is your Partner who creates growth. The two, man and Maker, working together in a beautiful eternal Partnership, fulfill the plan of the universe.

* * *

You learn the answer to the question: "How can you love your neighbor, let alone your enemy?" The answer is that it is futile even to try, if you are hoping to love in your own strength. But when you get yourself out of the way and let your Partner take over, you draw upon a supply of power infinitely greater that that possessed by all men. Then He, working through you, performs perfectly what is humanly impossible, even to the point of aiding your enemy. It is not you who loves the sinner; it is God within you. Just as the sun does not stop shining, God does not stop loving.

* * *

You learn that true education imparts to children the truth about the part the Creative Spirit plays in the sciences, in mathematics, in language, in every phase of learning. How can God be left out of any subject? If the work of the Creative Spirit is integrated with the acquired knowledge, the student gets a true and not a false education. He is equipped with the whole armor of God to meet life's struggles. As it is today, education often stuffs him with much knowledge and little understanding.

* * *

You learn that you don't have to be "rich." You don't have to be "born well." All you need is to get understanding and to sincerely put your understanding to work. Do this and all other things will be added unto you.

In seeking understanding, you are seeking God. In putting understanding to work, you have found God within you as your ever-present Partner. Your part in the Partnership is to be an instrument for God to work through. This does not require riches, position, noted ancestors or any of the other features usually associated with success. All you need for a really successful life is to work your partnership, keeping your Partner in the number one spot as Author, Sustainer and Source of Inspiration.

But there is a third party in this relationship: your fellow-man, whom *you learn* to embrace with love and understanding in the ordinary affairs of the workaday world. "He that loveth not his brother, whom he hath seen, how can he love God, whom he hath not seen?"

You learn that God within each of you manifests Himself through one person to another without need of spoken words. This is the Christ Spirit, the presence of God. This is what Christ came to teach you. This is what He gave His life for. He was man infused with God. He gave you not some abstract principle, but a living, everyday demonstration of the Partnership of man and Maker.

The Christ Spirit has existed from the beginning. Long before the coming of Jesus on earth, the prophets spoke of the coming of the Christ Spirit. It has always been present in the center of man. It is God seeking to express Himself in the infinite variety of human personalities. It is the Light and Life of every man that comes into the world.

The early Christians really possessed and were possessed by the Christ Spirit. The central challenge confronting you today is to recapture and be recaptured by the Christ Spirit. This is God's supreme gift to man. It is the gift of Himself.

* * *

You learn that the change in you is not an interruption of the normal; it is the breaking up of the abnormal. It is the disintegration of a symbol man has worshipped as the God of success. The impotence of that type of success is proved by the new you.

You have struck a tremendous bargain. You have traded in a petty, self-centered, unlovely ego for a divine-centered loving Higher Self. You have come upon that which makes great men great, their oneness with their Maker, their voluntary surrender of self.

As the huge oak lies waiting in the little acorn, as the ugly caterpillar carries within it the pattern of the exquisite butterfly, so within you is your Greater Self. Once you desire more than anything else to breathe out ego, breathe in God, the divine Power comes flooding in just as beautiful music floods a room when a radio is tuned in. And with it comes love greater than you ever dreamed, happiness and peace of mind beyond imagination.

* * *

You learn to seek your Partner's guidance at the day's beginning. Awakening in the morning, you take time out for a quiet period. You know that you are not alone. Welling within you is a deep sense of joy and gratitude for your Partner's many blessings. "Behold what manner of love the Father hath bestowed upon you." You reflect on His gifts of love: "Thank you, Father, for the night of rest and for its sweet restoring qualities. Thank you for another day, for the rising sun and the blue sky and the sweet invigorating air; for home and loved ones, for work to do, for food to eat, for friends to love—blessings without end."

This quiet time with your Partner sets the pattern for the day. He knows what the day will bring forth. He prepares you to take everything in stride. You will not be at the mercy of "breaks." You will have a

strength and peace of mind that cannot be destroyed
by man-made events.

* * *

You learn to gaze upon children with an entirely
new interest. The Power that created the child sustains it as its living Partner. The child senses this great
truth and in its early life lives entirely by guidance.
When it becomes old enough to acquire adult arro-
gance and pride, the child loses the truth. Could we
adults become as little children! Thomas Huxley
wrote: "Sit down before the facts as a little child, be
prepared to give up every preconceived notion, follow
humbly wherever Nature leads, or you shall learn nothing. I have only begun to learn content and peace of
mind since I have resolved at all risks to do this."

* * *

You learn to let your love go out to the derelict or
less fortunate one whose path crosses yours. Your
ray of light may keep alive in him the Inner Light's
last dying flame. Note the effects of love shown by an
old German to a young Negro attempting to escape
slavery. The boy was George Washington Carver, who
became one of America's greatest scientists, and who
went on to become one of God's most devoted partners.

Who knows the particular thing he was created to
do? The one thing you do know is that whatever it is
it can only be done with love. When you fail to give
love wherever the opportunity offers, you fail both

the person who needed your love and your Partner. You also fail yourself, for the one who benefits most when you give love selflessly is you. And the benefits extend to all eternity. "Give what you have," said Longfellow, "it may be better than you dare to think." And, "Little is much, if the heart be turned toward Heaven," says the Talmud.

* * *

You learn that you are really making no sacrifice in yielding your ego to God. Trading ego's 60 watt lamp for the illimitable Light of your Creative Partner is hardly a sacrifice. Your own little lamp gives out a light so dim that you and others like you keep crawling over one another. Your Partner's Light illuminates your whole life and shows you that the way to happiness is by helping one another. He offers you a real and important part to play in the Partnership. Without you, your Partner cannot do His work. Without Him, you are nothing. Together, He and you can do anything and everything.

* * *

You learn from your own past experience how easy it is for a man to give himself credit for skill in making or purchasing things at a price and selling them at a higher price. Yet this same man can be entirely oblivious of the infinite skill required to make a flower, to create a sunset, to control the ocean tides by the attraction of a moon 240,000 miles away, to grow beets and spinach and oranges and apples out of tiny seeds

and soil and water and sun and then to transform them
into blood and bone and muscle and brain.

What deadens your appreciation of these common
wonders? What permits you to exalt your own ego
over trifling accomplishments while remaining blind
to the miracles performed daily before your eyes by
Almighty God?

There are several answers. First, you have not been
adequately taught to know your living, working Partnership with the Creative Power. Out of the first reason flows the second: you have been taught to rise in
the world, to get somewhere, to do something, to be
somebody. To acknowledge the hand of God in your
accomplishments would be a bitter blow to pride. The
truth of God's greatness and your own littleness is
very difficult for ego to take. So your eyes are closed
to the truth and you bring upon yourself an abbrevi-
ated and frustrated life. Such a time calls for breathing out ego, breathing in God.

* * *

You learn that it is not really you that your friends
love and admire; it is the Light that shines through
you, your Partner's Light. Do you doubt it? Remember those times when your ego took command and
your Partner's Light could not be seen through you.
Were you lovable and admirable then? Yet such occasions serve a good purpose. They enable you to compare the reactions of others to ego and to the Light.
Thus you see truly that ego is nothing and the Light
is all.

You learn how subtly ego overcomes the person who persuades himself he can "worship" God without the need of giving himself up to God. He says to Christ: "I can be a Christian without doing it your way. I can hold to God with one hand and to ego with the other."

* * *

You learn the true significance of "Greater Love hath no man than this, that he lay down his life for his friends." Knowing that He was to be crucified on the morrow, what did Christ pray for? "Father, the hour is come. . . I pray that they all may be *one;* as Thou, Father, *art in me and I in Thee,* that they also may be *one* in us; that the world may believe Thou hast sent me. And the glory which Thou gavest me I have given them; that they may be *one,* even as we are *one.* . . *I in them and Thou in me, that they may be made perfect in one.* . ."

Oneness with God was the prayer with which Christ went to His death, the Partnership Life in action. The church of today can hardly dream of the support it would have from within and without if only it would come forth with a ringing call to the Partnership Life for which Christ lived and died. This is the church's supreme opportunity and responsibility, for despite its limitations, there is no other instrument as capable of restoring to groping humanity its divine and shining dream.

* * *

You learn that the critic of the church who sees in

it only a maze of rituals is blinding himself to the facts. If the Christian church did not have something more than rituals, if it did not have as its keystone the principles of Christ's way of life, could it possibly have survived twenty tumultous centuries?

* * *

You learn never to sit in judgment on your fellow-man's ways of achieving oneness with God. Yield the driver's seat to God, and you will have neither thought nor desire to judge someone else's religion. You will come to see in your fellow-man not one whose color, creed or race is different from your own, but one who has the same Partner as you have. Working your Partnership within the framework of your own church, you unconsciously encourage others to do likewise in their church.

* * *

You learn there is a simple test for any religious practice: Does it strengthen your ties with your Maker? Does it cause you to look for Him in every person you meet?

Some well-meaning folks decry all rituals as childish, unnecessary and even superstitious. Are these folks not forgetting the value of repetition in learning? Do they forget that constant repetition impressed things on their mind? *You learn* things by saying them and doing them over and over. *You learn* them by heart.

The problem is to do them *with* your heart.

If the ritual you practice helps you to work your

Partnership with God, then keep practicing it.

If the ritual serves to take the place of working your Partnership with God, then abandon it.

The Master followed certain rituals of the Jewish religion. But He fought strenuously against rituals becoming the central theme. When the Orthodox Church made the ritual virtually everything, Christ did not hesitate to condemn the practice as hypocritical.

The practice of breathing out ego, breathing in God can be construed as a ritual. Think what this practice does for you. You should never be persuaded to abandon it. The one purpose in life—the reason you were created—is to achieve oneness with your Maker. This is the one purpose, but there are countless ways to help you achieve it.

* * *

You learn never to be depressed by "bad" weather. You know that nobody could run the weather better than He who does run it. Think what would happen if men were given the same freedom to handle the weather that they have in their own affairs. You would have pressure groups from all parts of the country demanding things favorable to their particular desires. These pressure groups would be fighting other pressure groups and all would be fighting among themselves. Some would want the rain at a certain time of the morning; others would want it at night; still others would not want it to rain at all that day.

"Bad" weather helps you to appreciate the clear

days. How monotonous life would be if every day were sunny! You leave the weather, like everything else in your life, in your Partner's hands, not even silently wishing for a change. You know that "everything works for good for those who love the Lord."

* * *

You learn that there are times when the practice of breathing out ego, breathing in God, does not seem to work well. Even great prophets and saints pass through times when God seems far away. This lack of constancy is natural. You are a physical as well as a mental and spiritual being. If your physical body is not functioning properly, both mind and spirit can be adversely affected.

When you find it difficult to breathe in God, it might be well to seek the help of a trusted friend or an understanding minister, priest or rabbi. Try having a quiet time in church alone, or listen to some beautiful and inspiring music.

Perhaps you need to get away for awhile. A change may be indicated. This is not a sign of weakness. The Master often repaired to the mountains, and the Creator shows the importance of change in the multiplicity and variety of the creation—in the weather, in foods, in colors, in faces, in temperaments. Make sure the change you seek is not an escape. Find a retreat where you can relax and get close to God, face your troubles and turn them over to your Creative Partner. Meanwhile keep breathing out ego, breathing in God. Do

it with your mind as well as with your physical being. Gradually or suddenly the feeling of doubt and
depression will leave. The Spirit of your Partner will
fill you with His love and power, and your faith in
Him and in the Partnership Life will be stronger than
ever.

* * *

You learn that sometimes it is impossible to keep
wrong thoughts from entering your mind. *You learn*
not to worry about it, but simply to refuse hospitality
to the evil thoughts. You cannot get rid of them by
fiercely determining not to think of them. But there is
a natural and practical solution to the problem. By
the steady practice of breathing out ego, breathing in
God, the evil thoughts are swept out of your mind.
When your eyes and thoughts rest steadfastly on your
Partner, nothing evil can make headway with you.

* * *

You learn there are as many pathways to the Partnership Life as there are people treading them. Elimination of ego is required on each of these pathways.
St. John of the Cross said: "Absolute self-giving is
the only pathway from the human to the divine." While
the pathways differ in other respects, each is paved
with the desire to get self out of God's way. Suffering
often is such a pathway, but not if it is nothing more
than a protest against bitter circumstances. Suffering
can be creative only when you consent to it as part of
the Plan for your growth.

You learn that as you grow more and more aware of your Partnership, you are less inclined to chafe at the feeling that your part is an insignificant one. You know that there is a wide difference between God's sense of values and man's, and you are comforted by the fact that your Partner knows your willingness to serve in any capacity He chooses for you. It has been said that man is free only to choose his master. You have chosen your Master, and in order to keep mindful of your choice you practice breathing out ego, breathing in God.

* * *

You learn that without God's Presence what is called personality is mere tinsel. The most valuable instrument you can have at your disposal is your personality, but in order to put this instrument in tune, you need to let go and let God take over. Then you find yourself in tune not only with God but with His creatures and His world.

* * *

You learn that the Partnership life means more than giving God a mental wave of the hand on departing from church on Sunday, as if to say, "See you next week, same time, same place."

* * *

You learn that what the world needs is what each creature needs, understanding of the Presence of God in every situation. The world needs people who understand their Partnership with God, and who seek only to have Him work through them. Such people will work wherever they are; they will work with love and imagination, and patience, seeking creative answers. Many a fine project has been upset because someone has allowed ego to take over God's place. Even the most genuine and sincere enthusiasm can go astray if ego is not kept in full check. Hence the necessity that ego continually be breathed out and God regularly be breathed in.

* * *

You learn what to do when you are up against an "impossible" situation. Perhaps everything seems stacked against you: too much work, too much disharmony, too much pain. Possibly you have gotten out of the habit of breathing out ego, breathing in God. Maybe you even have forgotten God, and His Light seems not to shine for you. But the Inner Light sometimes shines brightest when the opening is tiniest. The sheer force of your sense of futility and despair can push you back to the only source that can help you. So you start again to breathe out ego, breathe in God, and again you are able to grow and to create. You do not attempt to bombard your way through. Instead you become calm and still, and He takes over.

* * *

You learn that you are the creation and expression of God; that you are not abandoned to your own resources; that God is part of you, directing your life and destiny. If you will, you can be delivered just as you are—frailties, suffering and all—into a certainty of your oneness with God, with other men, and with the universe. No longer will you roam the world looking in vain for some one or some plan to save you from loneliness or insecurity. You will have found the answer in the Presence of God, your Partner.

You know that the great secret of unity with God is kept from men only until it becomes their soul's sincere desire above all else. You feel a deep desire to help men to get this understanding.

* * *

You learn that almost everyone is an "alcoholic" of a sort—one whose desires in a certain direction have gone out of bounds. There is the money alcoholic, the sex alcoholic, the power alcoholic, the publicity alcoholic, the eating alcoholic.

Alcoholics Anonymous has done such a magnificent job because each member *knows* that he of himself is powerless; that God alone can help him. Why should alcoholics of another sort feel so respectable and look down upon the liquor alcoholic? Every sincere member of Alcoholics Anonymous lives the Partnership Life, and carries with him the presence of God. Is that not the answer to all forms of alcoholism?

* * *

You learn that the priceless factor in a product is the love that goes into its making. This priceless factor cannot be purchased with money or any material commodity. It is born of contented workers, well paid, respected and appreciated, who are convinced their work is worth while and rendering a service to humanity. The priceless factor, being love, cannot be put into a product unless there is love from the factory head down to the factory worker. With such a product, the purchase price becomes secondary, for its quality is so outstanding it stands alone.

* * *

You learn wholeness and balance. When God created in man His image, He gave you wholeness and balance. He meant you to be sound physically, mentally and spiritually. If you follow His guidance, you will maintain this wholeness and balance. But if you violate His simple laws for the body, you create an imbalance and there is no wholeness. You may feed your mind and spirit on inspiring thoughts and selfless motives, but you must also feed your body the natural life-giving elements your Maker placed in His foods.

People can feel insecure because of a lack of love—a spiritual element; but they can also feel insecure because of a lack of natural life-giving food—a physical element. There is one natural source of supply for all your hidden hungers, the Source that gave you life and that sustains that life from day to day, from hour to hour and from minute to minute.

You are not to say to your Creative Partner: "I shall follow you in things of the mind and spirit, but I cannot believe you expect me to be so mundane as to be mindful of the food I eat. If I eat foods that have been robbed of their life-giving elements, I expect not to suffer." You must come to your Partner in total commitment, and then you find His abundance pressed down and running over. He works only in wholeness and balance. "Thy faith hath made thee whole." A complete faith, that is, not a two-thirds one.

* * *

You learn how to accept criticism. This is a free country and probably in no respect is freedom exercised more than to criticise. Of the 160 million people in the country, most have not been given to understand that God is within them—an ever-present working Partner. Lacking this belief, they feel free to criticise their fellow-man. It is an expensive and destructive indulgence, engaged in everywhere, indoors and outdoors. Where two or three are gathered together, too often there will be criticism. Some of this will surely be directed at you. This should come as no surprise when it is remembered that even the Founder of Christianity was not spared. No one knew better how to take criticism than the Master. So selfless was He that even on the cross He was able to say, "Forgive them, Father, for they know not what they do."

* * *

You learn that when you capture the Partnership idea, power comes to you. It is said that a man can be reformed only by a new idea which commands his own. The Partnership concept is such an idea. When you un-

derstand that God is your Partner, you realize you are
not so much a workman in the world as a suggestion
of what you are yet to be. You walk as a prophecy of
the next age.

* * *

You learn that your greatest enemy is ego and that
ego's greatest weapon is fear. Fear convinces you that
you have much more than your share of things to do,
and you don't see how you will ever get them done.
Fear causes you to grow weary, weak, exhausted, so
that you just can't go on. Fear talks you into a breakdown. Some people say that if you can be talked into
a breakdown you can be talked into a build-up. But
the build-up is there within you, if you will only let it
work for you. Breathing out ego, breathing in God, is
the way. The build-up then is not the result of talking
yourself into anything. It is real, because it comes
from God, and God is real. Paul said, "I can do all
things through Him that strengtheneth me." Everyone who has tried to let God have His way knows that
God strengthens him.

Fear would have you believe you are unequal to
your responsibilities. But God and you as partners
are more than a match for anything. Some say, "Accen-
tuate the positive in your thinking and the positive
will be accentuated in your living." This is fine if you
can do it, but sometimes it is like trying to lift yourself by your own bootstraps. The positive is in you
all the time in the Presence of God; all you have to
do if you want it to work is to get out of its way.

Breathe out ego, breathe in God—and mean it. Then you come under the influence of the Power and Love which banish all fear.

* * *

You learn that even Christ was tempted to divide his allegiance between ego and God. It would have been easy for a man of His talents to ally Himself with the priests or the scholars of His day. And consider the pressure upon Him to establish a political kingdom and thus bring relief to His people. His life was a decisive battle between ego and God, culminating in the ultimate choice in the Garden of Gethsemane. Only a sure and steady realization of God's presence within Him saw Him through. In His firm decisions, in the finality of His resolutions, in the clearness of His perceptions, we see one who was sure of Himself because He knew God was working through Him.

* * *

You learn the significance of circles. St. Augustine described the nature of God as a circle whose center is everywhere and whose circumference is nowhere. In one view, the eye is the first circle; the second is the horizon formed by the eye. Everywhere in nature this primary figure is repeated without end. Around every circle another can be drawn, as rings indicating a tree's growth. There is no end in nature, because every apparent end is really a beginning. The circle indicates immortality.

Thought waves travel in circles. Every thought

must eventually complete the circle and affect the thinker. This is the principle of loving thought,—it returns to the sender, enriched many times. But it is equally true of the hate thought,—the hater hurts himself most of all. If you hate the Russian people, the hate comes back to you. In rejecting and opposing communism, you are not to hate the people who foolishly are communists.

God loves you, and you complete the circle when your love goes back to Him. So it is clear why ego must not lead. The ways of self are selfish ways. The thoughts of self are selfish thoughts. They must complete their circle by harming you. But when you submerge your will in your Partner's Will, He inspires in you thoughts of selfless love which travel the full circle and in the course of time come back to bless you.

* * *

You learn how to free your mind from negative, inharmonious, destructive thoughts and from fears and doubts. You learn how to meet the overburdening cares, pains and heartaches that threaten to engulf you and force you to give way under the strain. You deal with them by the simple, common-sense realization that you do not stand alone, that you have a Partner with whom all things are possible and who "knoweth what things you have need of before you ask Him." He who has kept your heart going during the night, who sustains you every minute of the day, is not unmindful of all your other needs.

He knows all about your frustrations. He will not permit you to be taxed beyond your ability to withstand. If you get self out of the way long enough, certain of these frustrations will turn out to be blessings. But if you ignore your Partner's Presence, if you insist on carrying your burdens alone, you are headed for a breakdown.

So breathe out ego, breathe in God. "Above all the grace and gifts that Christ gave to His beloved," said St. Francis of Assisi, "is that of overcoming self." In losing self you find your Divine Self. In giving up ego, you find God. In your Partner's good time, life's most wonderful gifts come gravitating to you. Love, happiness, friends, achievement, peace of mind flow toward you in an irresistible stream. To those in the grip of self, this is unbelievable; freed of self, you will know that nothing is more real.

* * *

You learn that knowing how to handle your troubles does not mean that they will disappear. It does mean that you have taken them out of the hands of self and put them in your Partner's hands.

The way of self is to puff up small difficulties to balloon size, to take "a pile of dirt where gophers sit and make a mountain of it." Self gets upset over things so small they should be despised and forgotten. Self magnifies them so that you cannot work or sleep. Self is that amazing paradox, the least thing in the world trying to be the greatest thing in the world.

You know men whose self goes into a rage if bugs eat their flowers. Others go into tantrums or clench their teeth fighting to restrain a vicious outburst of temper simply because in a game supposedly played for fun a little white ball just misses falling into a hole. Others go into a fit of despondency because an expected letter or phone call does not arrive. These are manifestations of self in action.

What is the answer? It is not in urging self to think positive and constructive thoughts. It is in turning your affairs over to your Partner. So breathe out ego, breathe in God—for God *is* the answer.

* * *

You learn that there are hidden joys in eating. All food is a gift from your Partner. True, you have had a hand in earning it, and others have had a hand in preparing it. But the pleasure of eating is all yours. Suppose yours were also the chore of digesting the food and transforming it into blood, bone, muscle, and brain. But your Partner does all this for you. He gives you the fun of eating, while He does the chores. He does all the vital work and allows you all the fun. Pretty soft! How could you be less than deeply grateful for a set-up like that?

As you eat, your thoughts turn to the miracle of rebuilding that is going on within you. The bringing in of new material, the hauling away of waste. All being done not *by* you but *for* you. You ponder on the magical way in which proteins, mineral salts, vitamins, carbohydrates and all other necessary elements are being furnished your body out of the food you enjoy eating.

You come upon another great discovery. These physical elements, marvelous as they are and necessary to your well-being, are no more vital than the amazing spiritual elements God has placed in His natural foods. The spiritual substances, however, can give you their best *only if you recognize their presence*. They need your understanding and gratitude to complete the work. God's plan clearly is to supply food for the entire man, for body, mind and spirit. When you become conscious of the spiritual aspect of the whole process, certain potential qualities in your food are set free, and these nourish, revive and bless you. When you eat God's food thoughtfully, blessing each mouthful, the food tastes better; it is digested more readily; and there is no logy or sleepy feeling after eating. Your mind is clearer and more alert. You are a better instrument for your Partner.

You resolve that never again will you thoughtlessly bolt your food. Never again will you eat while under nervous strain. You will do without food rather than eat when upset.

Eating is a great example of the Partnership Life in action. Both Partners are indispensable to this vital function. Several times each day, you and your Creative Partner work together to effect one of life's great miracles. The grace you now offer before each meal, with or without words, takes on a form and beauty that strengthen and glorify your Partnership with God.

* * *

You learn not to look back on yesterday with regret or upon tomorrow with fear, because the mind that is cluttered with remorse for the past or foreboding for the future cannot be open to the great possibilities of today. The Light is obscured from the eye that strains backward to yesterday or projects its anxiety toward the morrow. But eternal Truth is revealed to the eye that is single in its focus on God's Presence here and now—today.

This is not a philosophy of "eat, drink and be merry" or of idle drifting. It is pin-pointed concentration on doing what is expected of you *now* by your Partner—a receptive open-mindedness to His guidance and inspiration, which keeps you tuned to life's true rhythm. You learn to forget time and to live in the eternal where God is. When He is with you, anxieties and fears have no power over you.

* * *

You learn the greatness of simplicity. The Master selected simple, unlearned men for His disciples. In order to understand the Partnership Life a man must possess two simple qualities, an open mind and a desire to know the truth. Self-satisfied and proud men employ physical power and material resources to secure and maintain high position in the eyes of the world. But the simple man who understands the source of all power depends entirely on the Presence of God within him.

You learn, when a crisis breaks your accustomed routine, not to act before you think. The ego tends to act automatically, leaping before looking. But the new you, though dazed and possibly bewildered by an emergency, acts quite differently. You become still, absolutely quiet. You breathe out self and breathe in God. Even when fear swells to terror, when pain attacks without warning, when a series of untoward events threatens to overwhelm your courage and crush your hope, you learn to stay composed. And in the few moments of breathing in God, you are told what to do.

An easy solution may not be forthcoming. The difficult situation must be faced. But peace of mind and wisdom have been given you. Others, led by self, may lose their heads in the crisis. Their houses have been built on sand, not on the rock of partnership with God. When you become still you deny fear the power to panic you. And while you are still and breathing out self, God comes in. It is a simple operation of the Great Law,—let go and let God take over.

You do not tell others to be still. You simply let go yourself. They may learn the truth from observation. You do not say: "See what I have overcome; note how cheerful I am; observe how completely I have mastered these dark events." If you must remind people of dark events, you have not really overcome them.

* * *

You learn to stay calm in all kinds of stress—fear, anger, uncertainty, impatience, accident, defeat. To prevent ego from projecting itself into the situation and making a bad thing worse, you are quiet. Your regular habit of breathing out self, breathing in God, stands you in good stead.

Letting go and letting God take over works also in times of weakness, temptation, routine monotony, and excitement. At no time is it more helpful than when you are flushed with success or fame and the feeling of personal elation might overcome you.

"This, too, shall pass" applies to your moments of victory as well as to your moments of trial. Faith in your Partner's Presence and in His control of your affairs gives you true confidence and peace of mind.

* * *

You learn the advanced step of breathing out love to others, breathing in God's love for you.

When you are able to forget self and to breathe out love to all mankind, there is no limit to the blessing you are broadcasting. It radiates in all directions. It travels through the realm of Spirit; it is not confined by the physical atmosphere; it is not limited by distance; it contacts the spiritual nature of all who are receptive to it. Marvelous results are thus accomplished.

And the great miracle is the return of these blessings to the one giving them out. The more you send out, the greater will be your ability to both receive and broadcast blessings. You become a channel for your Creator to heal and to prosper.

* * *

You learn that your Partner has left you free to

head your Partnership, should you so decide. But common sense should keep you from abusing this freedom. Voluntarily you surrender it to your Partner. "Not my will, but Thine."

This decision is the keystone of your future. It is the most important decision of your life; no other will ever approach it in significance or rewards. Having done this one thing, you have in effect done everything. You have made the eternal Creative Power the head of your Partnership, and He never makes mistakes.

You will continue to make mistakes, because sometimes you will take the leadership from Him. He freely permits you to do this. He does more, He forgives you these trespasses. As you learn that these excursions of the ego inevitably get you into trouble, they become less frequent.

The decision to give back to God the freedom He gave you is sometimes described as "conversion," "being born anew," "being made over," "losing your life in order to find it," "accepting last place and ending up in first place." But it all begins with common sense, because it lets Him run the Partnership Who is without question qualified to do so. Having tried out both partners in the number one spot, you know from hard practical experience which One belongs there.

* * *

You learn that you cannot work your Partnership by evading the world. But with your Partner you can overcome the world by meeting everyday matters forthrightly and letting Him guide you in every thought and need. Christ, who made clear the Partnership of man and Maker, did not separate Himself from worldly affairs. He chose to live and do His work in the midst of them.

* * *

You learn proof of your originality. No one is like you—the whole world over. No one has your job to do. Look at the billions of snow flakes—none are alike. Each has its own originality. Does your Maker hold you in less respect than a snowflake? Look at the billions of leaves as they fall to earth. No two are alike. You also learn from these beautifully colored and enchanting leaves that God meant death to be beautiful.

* * *

You learn that there is one basic sin: separation from your Partner. All other sins stem from this one. If you remained united with God, making Him the fountainhead of all thought and action, you could not sin. You need to have only one concern, to remain a channel through which your Partner's grace may flow.

* * *

You learn that without the understanding of his Creative Partner's presence, man has his limitations. And once people find that their idol has limitations, it is all over with him. What matter that he has talent, enterprise or knowledge? The glitter that surrounded him yesterday looks tarnished today.

How different with him who knows that of himself he is nothing, but that the Light within him is everything! One cannot help take note of him. The best hopes of mankind, their deepest spiritual convictions, rest upon such a man. In his mind, one senses a new influx of divinity. Because the great Creative Spirit is being given free play, man is given heart.

* * *

You learn that it is not enough to look upon your past mistakes with remorse and to consider this sufficient. Repentance that does not result in actual day-to-day working of your partnership in deeds of love for your fellow-man can end in smugness and self-deception.

* * *

You learn these things about immortality: Your Maker and Partner placed definite yearnings within you, and for each yearning He supplied the fulfillment. You thirst for water; He supplied the natural springs from which waters burst forth. You crave air; from mountains and plains and oceans air comes flowing into your lungs. You hunger for food; the earth's bosom yields the fruits and vegetables, grains and meat you need. Is there a greater yearning man has than for immortality? Surely your Maker has in store for those who strive for oneness with Him the immortality they crave. Yours is the responsibility of becoming worthy. "Immortality will come to such as are fit for it, and he who would be a great soul in the future, must be a great soul now." In the transformation of the worm into the butterfly, we see the promise of man's immortality. There could be no butterfly unless the worm were transmuted. Wings come after the earthly body has passed away.

* * *

You learn that the things you love most in your loved ones may be clearer in their absence, as the mountain is clearer to the climber from the plain.

* * *

You learn, when a loved one passes from your sight, he becomes, like the tie between you, invisible. But is the tie not felt even more strongly than when your loved one walked among you in the flesh? And is not this your Partner's doing? Neither He nor the tie nor the love can be seen. But the love lives and grows and goes on loving forever. To your limited vision, death seems death. To your Partner, it is daybreak, the fulfillment of night that a new dawn might appear, a dawn of release and freedom and joy.

Science, once considered as disbelieving what it could not see, recently has been moving toward an acceptance of the existence and power of the spirit. Science knows that body cells are always dying. The body-substance you call yours today was not yours a year ago. The brain of which you feel so proud was not with you a few months before. If the brain and the whole body can die and disappear many times during life itself, while memory and personality remain through the various changes and deaths, is it not reasonable to assume that when the last of your body has disappeared, your identity will still live on in the

Spirit in which your Partner works? As He is eternal, so, too, are His creatures who have lived in His Love and Spirit.

Faith, hope, and love are realities, but they are outside the physical. They come from the same Creator who gave you life, but they are not of the body that finally passes on, not of the materials which make up the earth.

Love is the foundation and keystone of life. Is Love's creation really broken by the body's death? Just as, in Washington's words, "It is impossible to reason without arriving at a Supreme Being," so it is irrational to assume that your Creator would permit the destruction of His own work.

Benjamin Franklin said: "And when I observe that there is great frugality, as well as wisdom, in His works. . . when I see nothing annihilated, and not even a drop of water wasted, I cannot suspect the annihilation of souls, or believe that He will suffer the daily waste of millions of minds ready made that now exist, and put Himself to the continual trouble of making new ones. Thus finding myself to exist in the world, I believe I shall, in some shape or other, always exist; and with all the inconveniences human life is liable to, I shall not object to a new edition of mine; hoping, however, that the errata of the last may be corrected. . ."

* * *

Christ gave you evidence of immortality not only in His words but in His deeds and in His life, "I go to prepare a place for you. . . that where I am, there ye may be also. . . except a corn of wheat fall into the

ground and die, it abideth alone. But if it die, it bringeth forth much fruit. . . Because I live, ye shall live
also. I am the resurrection and the life. . . Whosoever
liveth and believeth in Me shall never die. He that believeth in My way of life, the works that I do shall
he do also, and greater works than these shall he do. . ."

These words of the Master cannot be taken lightly
even by the skeptic steeped in unbelief. Is it reasonable
to believe that One who spent His entire life selflessly
making others happy—teaching, loving, helping, sacri-
ficing—would at the same time be betraying those He
was serving? The way He lived and died adds strength
to a conviction that He realized His immortality with
a certainty that death could not shake.

Among Christ's disciples and followers before His
death were men of various classes and occupations.
They were sane and honest, controlled in their move-
ments, careful in their judgments. While following
the Master in His earthly life, they were often subject
to doubts, vacillations and denials. But observe the
amazing transition in them after they had witnessed
the resurrection. Forthrightly and steadfastly they declared what they had seen and heard, adhering to their
story at the price of persecution, torture and death. *Do
men deliberately create a lie just to die for it?*

You are immortal from the instant you accept,
within your mind and soul, the Partnership with your
Maker. The Creator is immortal, and everything that
belongs to Him is immortal. And He is the other member of your Partnership.

Too Late, You Say?

Too late, you say? You've missed your chance? No, there is no such thing as a "last chance" in your Partner's plan. He is open to you at all times. What if you have sinned? Who hasn't? Is there not more rejoicing in heaven over one sinner who repents and seeks the Father than over many who feel they have not sinned? Seek God and you will know that heaven is within you. You will know that your understanding has been limited by your personal self which saw only material things. In the land of your Partner the outlook has no limitations.

It is as though you read in your morning paper that a great estate had been left to you. All you need to do is present your claim to it. This is really true: you file your claim by breathing out ego and breathing in God—and meaning it.

"A highway shall be there, and a way, and it shall be called the way of wholeness." The Spirit of your Partner is the spirit of wholeness. No horizon can limit you because God is in you, you are in Him, and He is everywhere. And His pleasure is to give you true happiness. Christ said, "It is your Father's good pleasure to give you the Kingdom."

And in your own times Kahlil Gibran has written: "Go to your fields and gardens, and you shall learn that it is the pleasure of the bee to gather honey of the flower. But it is also the pleasure of the flower to yield its honey to the bee. For to the bee, a flower is a fountain of life. And to the flower, the giving and the receiving of pleasure is a need and an ecstasy."

Let your Partner guide you and you will realize that there is no separation between man and his Maker. You are His hands and feet. He needs you to do His work. *But know your place, and know His place.* Let Him lead who should lead.

Make your resolution right now—today—to work your Partnership with Him, to get your inspiration and guidance direct from Him. Breathe out ego, breathe in God. Breathe out weakness, breathe in strength. Breathe out boredom, breathe in ecstasy.

All good things come from your Partner. Open the way and He will flood you with gifts. He will make you a channel for blessings to others. There will be a new power in you, a power you never dreamed of. Use it for the glory of your Maker to restore faith and well-being to others, so that they also may work their Partnership with God.

Too late, you say? Nothing is ever too late for your Partner. Nothing is ever impossible for Him. Hear the words of Browning's Rabbi Ben Ezra:

> Grow old with me,
> The best is yet be,
> The last of life,
> For which the first was made.
> Our times are in His hand
> Who saith "A whole I planned;
> Youth shows but half. Trust God; see all, nor be
>   afraid."

Trust God and He will strengthen your body and renew your mind. All things are new to him who renews his mind in Partnership with the Creator. Everything shines with a new radiance when you realize His presence within you. Old things become beautiful new discoveries. Gold hidden in a vein of ore for centuries is new to the prospector who finds it. Your Creator's Truth is continually new to him who continually discovers it. In him it becomes new life.

Too late, you say? You are too old? Might die—soon? Do you really think this existence is all there is? Would it be fair and just of the Creator to call everything quits and to leave you bereft of hope for something better? Look into life and you will find that it moves not in broken lines but in cycles. What better way to prepare for the next cycle than to work your Partnership with God while you are here on earth? Return to Him who made you and sent you forth, for He will be waiting for your return, to start you off on an even greater experience.

> If thou return to the Almighty, thou shall be built up.
> Acquaint now thyself with Him, and be at peace
> And the Almighty will be thy treasure,
> And precious silver unto thee.
> For then shalt thou delight thyself in the Almighty.
> And shalt lift up thy face unto God.
> Thou shalt make thy prayer unto Him, and He shall hear thee;
> And thou shalt pay thy vows.
> Thou shalt also decree a thing, and it shall be established unto thee;
> And light shall shine upon thy ways.

Return now to your home with God. Close your eyes a moment and be alone with your Partner. He is telling you it is never too late. Tell Him it is your soul's sincere desire that He take over the guidance of your life. He will know you mean it. Breathe out ego, and your Partner will come in. And He will be with you forever.